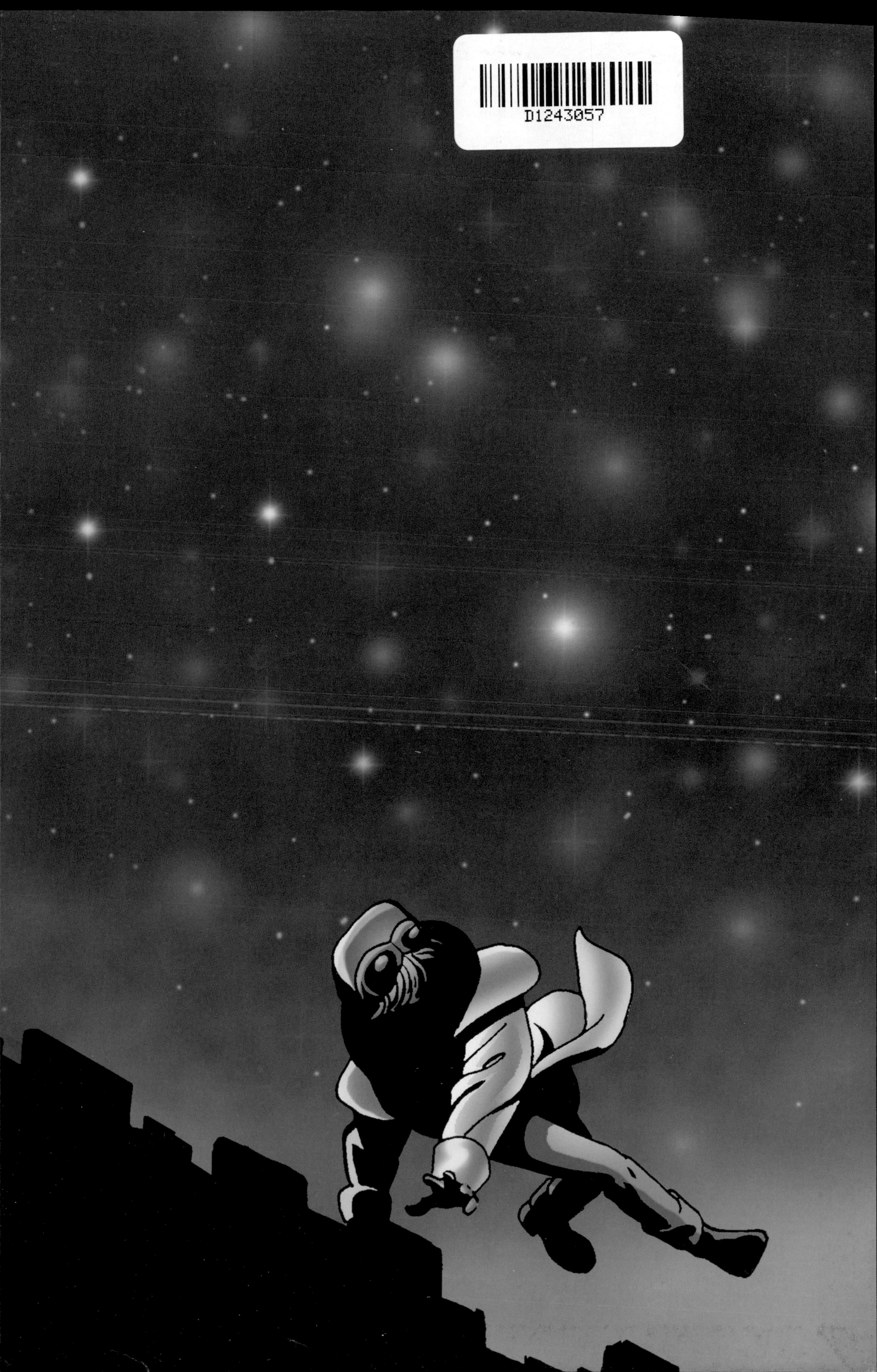

LEAVE IT TO CHANCE

ROBINSON • SMITH • FREEMAN • COX

image®

JAMES ROBINSON & PAUL SMITH

WITH

GEORGE FREEMAN
INKS

JEROMY COX
COLOR ART

AND

AMIE GRENIER
LETTERING

image®

LEAVE IT TO CHANCE VOL III: MONSTER MADNESS AND OTHER STORIES. Published by Image Comics, 1071 N. Batavia St. Ste. A, Orange, CA 92867. Image and its logos are ® and © 2003, Image Comics, inc. Copyright © 2003 by James Robinson and Paul Smith. All rights reserved. Originally published in single magazine format as LEAVE IT TO CHANCE Vol. III #9-11. LEAVE IT TO CHANCE, its logos, symbols, prominent characters featured in this volume and the distinctive likeness thereof, are trademarks of James Robinson and Paul Smith. Any similarities to persons living or dead is unintentional and purely coincidental. With the exception of artwork for review purposes, none of the contents of this pubication may be reprinted without the express permission of James Robinson and Paul Smith. PRINTED IN HONG KONG

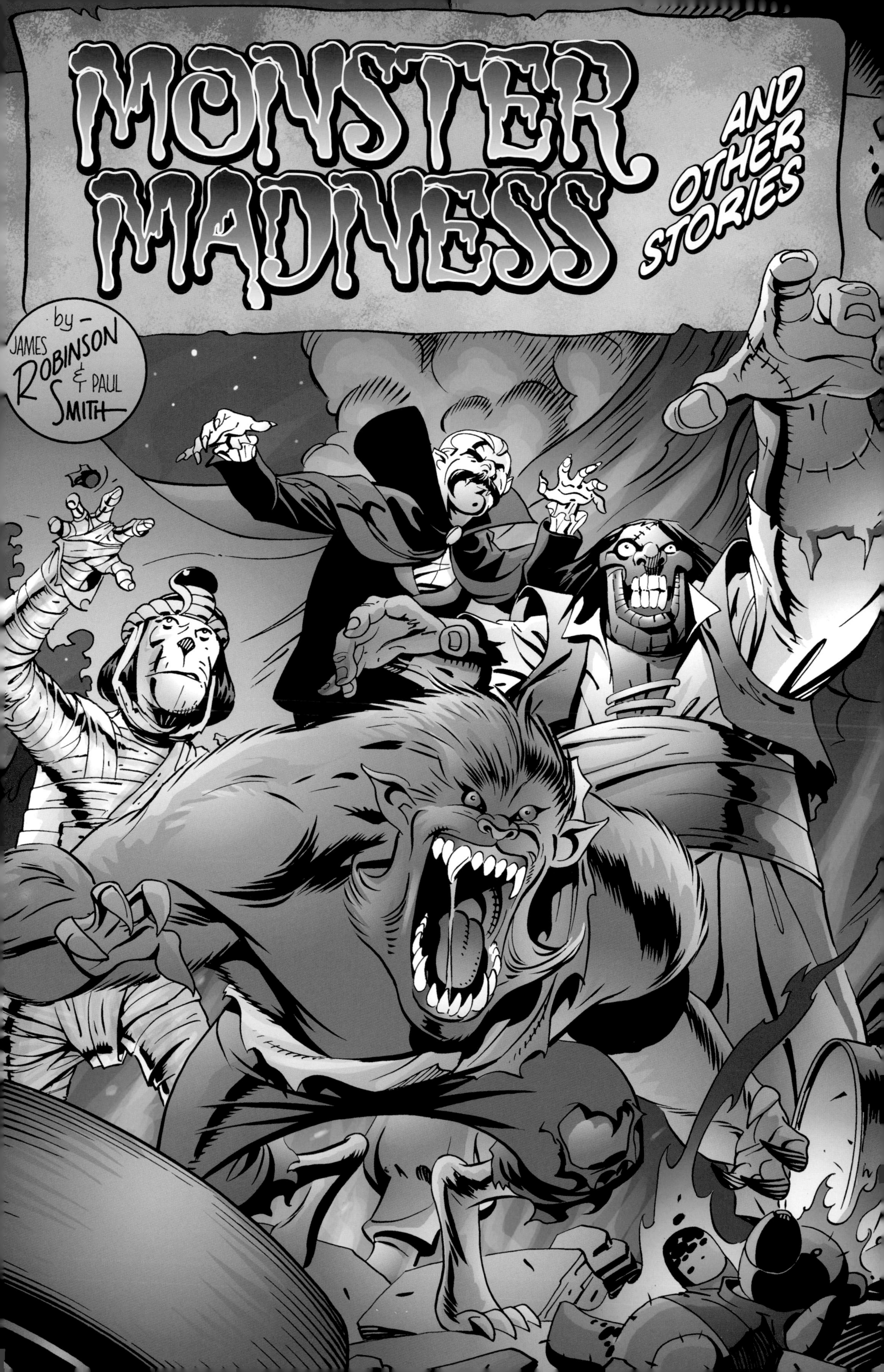
MONSTER MADNESS
AND OTHER STORIES
by
JAMES ROBINSON & PAUL SMITH

BIOGRAPHIES

JAMES ROBINSON

James Robinson came into America from the cold, gray climes of England. He stumbled into comic books like a drunken sailor and among his many works, most notable are The Golden Age, Firearm, WildC.A.T.s, Batman: Legends of the Dark Knight, 67 Seconds, London's Dark, Bluebeard and Illegal Alien. He recently finished his seven year opus Starman for DC Comics.

At the same time, James has entered the film world, adapting the League of Extraordinary Gentlemen for 20th Century Fox starring Sean Connery.

He resides in Hollywood.

PAUL SMITH

The victim of an abnormally happy childhood, the artist was born on 9/4/53 in Kansas City, Missouri, the youngest of three boys.

A former animator and storyboard artist (now in recovery), he has pretended to be a comics professional since the early 80's. Some of his various works include his rookie year on the X-Men, Dr. Strange, Mike Mahogany, Nexus, and The Golden Age (the latter in collaboration with James Robinson).

Highly opinionated and a royal pain to work with, the artist resides in southern California with his motorcycle, Lockheed. He has never met a deadline in his life.

GEORGE FREEMAN

George Freeman has been penciling, inking and colouring comics from his wintry Canadian home for the last twenty-four years.
Starting with Captain Canuck, he has since drawn Black Widow, Elric, Batman, Green Lantern, Jack of Hearts, Mr. Monster, The Challengers of the Unknown and various Big Book stories. In 1996, he and his wife, colourist Laurie E. Smith, were nominated for an Eisner Award for colouring the X-Files comic book. (Chris Ware won.)
He still enjoys Acme Novelty Library, British Mac magazines, Frank Giacoia inks and red-headed women.

JEROMY COX

Jeromy worked for four years as an animator for film, television, and video game projects. Jeromy started coloring comics for Wildstorm three years ago and hasn't stopped since.

Jeromy's self published comic book, Zombie Love, is on hiatus because he's working so much. Plans are to resume production later this year. Jeromy is currently coloring Leave it to Chance, Mage The Hero Defined, and is the Art Director on a super secret virtual reality project for Angel studios.

He likes bacon, coca cola, red vines, butterfingers, Star Wars and mayonnaise. Not necessarily in that order.

CONTENTS

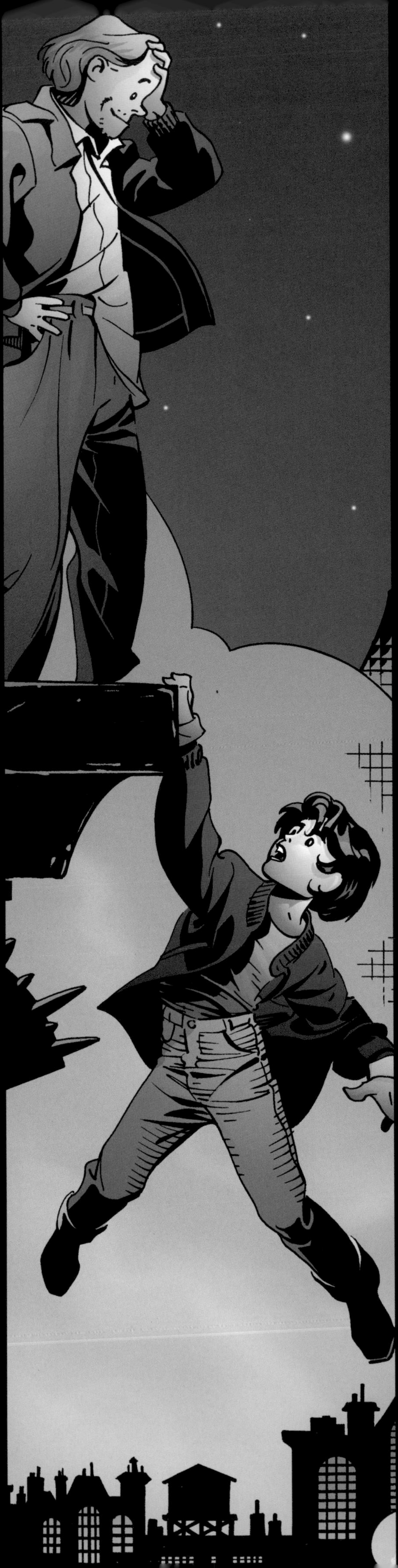

INTRODUCTIO

Time. It's been on my mind lately, thinkin about life and fate and one's place in the worlc I know that's an odd way to start this intro bu there you go. Let me run with it for a bit an we'll see how gracefully I can wrap this all up i a pretty pink package.

Wow, Volume Three of Leave It To Chance, fina ly. The stories you are about to read were neve collected before this time. Seeing it on the she beside the first two volumes I know will give m no end of delight, not only because this is the first time in hardcover, but also because they ar stories I have a huge amount of affection for.

The Monster Madness two-part tale is possibly m favorite story to date. I don't know, the whol idea of marrying the horror films of yore wi Woody Allen's Purple Rose of Cairo was a simpl concept that in many ways personified ever thing I wanted to do with Chance. It was fu exciting, all the major characters got the chance to shine, including Lucas who did mor than simply find out what Chance had been u to at the end of the story. He's supposed to b the occult investigator of Devil's Echo and he ge to find the solution to the drama, while h daughter got to do her own thing. I love th sense of urgency and how everything going c for all the characters at the same time ups th stakes but doesn't make it confusing.

I love Paul Smith's art in this story too. Don't ge me wrong, I've loved every issue he's done, b there's something about the images in this ta that captures my fancy.

Another aspect to note was that Roger, th unfortunate cop who becomes a werewolf serie regular, is base on a real gu (at least f the part

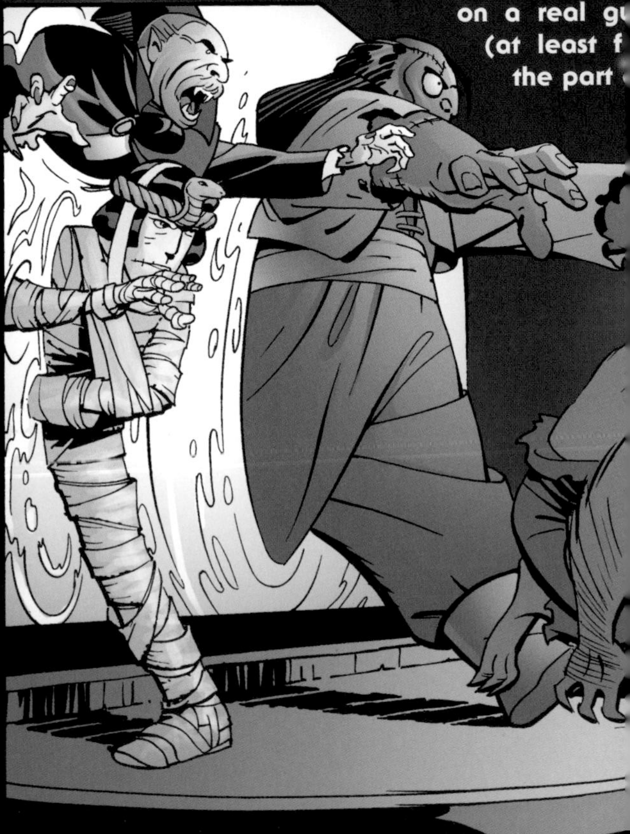

ne story where Roger the cop was human). I began auc-
oning off charity appearances in comic books back at a
otor City Con many years ago. On two separate occa-
ons I featured small characters in the pages of Starman,
e other comic I'm known for, who were modeled in
erms of their likeness on real life comic fans who had
iven money at these charity auctions. And even though
ese people I think assumed they'd be given a walk on
ole, I endeavored to give them a little bit more and
eature them in little sequences where they might shine.

ne same was true of Roger, who bid for and won an
ppearance in Chance. At the time Paul and I didn't
now what we were going to do with him. We certainly
idn't think we'd make him into a werewolf. We
bsolutely certainly didn't think he'd become a recurring
haracter in his wolfen form. But there you are.

ne hockey story is another favorite, because Paul and I
ot to play with the bizarre internal logic of a city where
e occult and the fantastic are the norm. I mean where
 the hockey rule-book does it say that a player has to
e alive to play the game? And again, Paul's art ruled.

hope you'll enjoy the stories as much as I do.

nd as I muse on this book and the stories therein, time
omes to mind constantly. Where did all that time go? I
as living a different life when these stories were writ-
en. Married in the suburbs. A comic book writer first
nd foremost. Life was simple.

ow I'm single, living in the heart of the city and
lthough I continue to love comic books, my primary
ource of writing work comes from screenplays. And my
fe is crazy. Time flies, and I look at my accomplish-
nents and see how few I've managed to achieve com-
ared to the grand dreams of feats galore I saw in my
uture back when I was a husband in cozy calm Burbank.
don't think I'm a failure, per se, but I know I'm by no
neans a success. My triumphs are small ones and within
ne world of comics my light of notoriety is very much on
ne decline. Which after all is how it should be. Creative
elds are transitory. Talents wax and wane, come and
go. There are young guys in comics now doing amazing writing, and I'm far more thrilled reading their efforts than strug-gling away at my own.

However, this leads back to Chance, a series I've always felt I did when I was cooking with the most creative gas I could muster. I've written before about that X factor that some writer/artists teams have. By themselves these creators are good even great, together they add an indefinable something to the mixture that makes the sum total greater than the parts. I honestly feel Smitty and I are one of those teams. It's always a joy to work with him, see the art for the first time, hear all his notions and ideas and additional bits of stuff he puts into the work. These three issues of Chance when I feel we really started getting our act down, especially reflect this.

It makes me pause to reflect on life then, working on Chance and my hopes for the series. I wonder what Roger and the other people I featured in charity cameos are doing now. One of the guys who bid for and won an appearance in Starman wanted his wife and baby son featured instead of himself. I ended up featuring all three of them as a family. I wonder how they are. The boy must be 5 or 6 by now. Walking, talking.

Yes, time has passed, but the stories you hold in your hands resonate for me. I look back on these as among the best I've done. Comic books are an interesting medium, because you have to produce them (when working on a monthly schedule/paying the monthly credit cards) at a fair clip. For this reason some of the work is good, some bad. Some of it you're proud of, some of it you wince to be reminded of when someone brings a copy for you to sign at a convention. I've been lucky, whether the public has liked much that I've done, I at least take pride in a few things. 67 Seconds, Illegal Alien, some Firearms, some Starmans, the Golden Age, and Leave It To Chance.

The last two projects were Paul Smith and I working together with all the burners on. I'm very grateful to have met Paul. Despite the traumas, the disappearances, the ups and down of working with a volatile creative force, I always came away from it knowing we had helped each other to do our best work.

Time passes. But I hope ten years from now, Paul and I are still working together in some capacity, still cooking with gas. And I hope that project continues to be the adventures of Chance Falconer.

James Robinson, Hollywood, 2003.

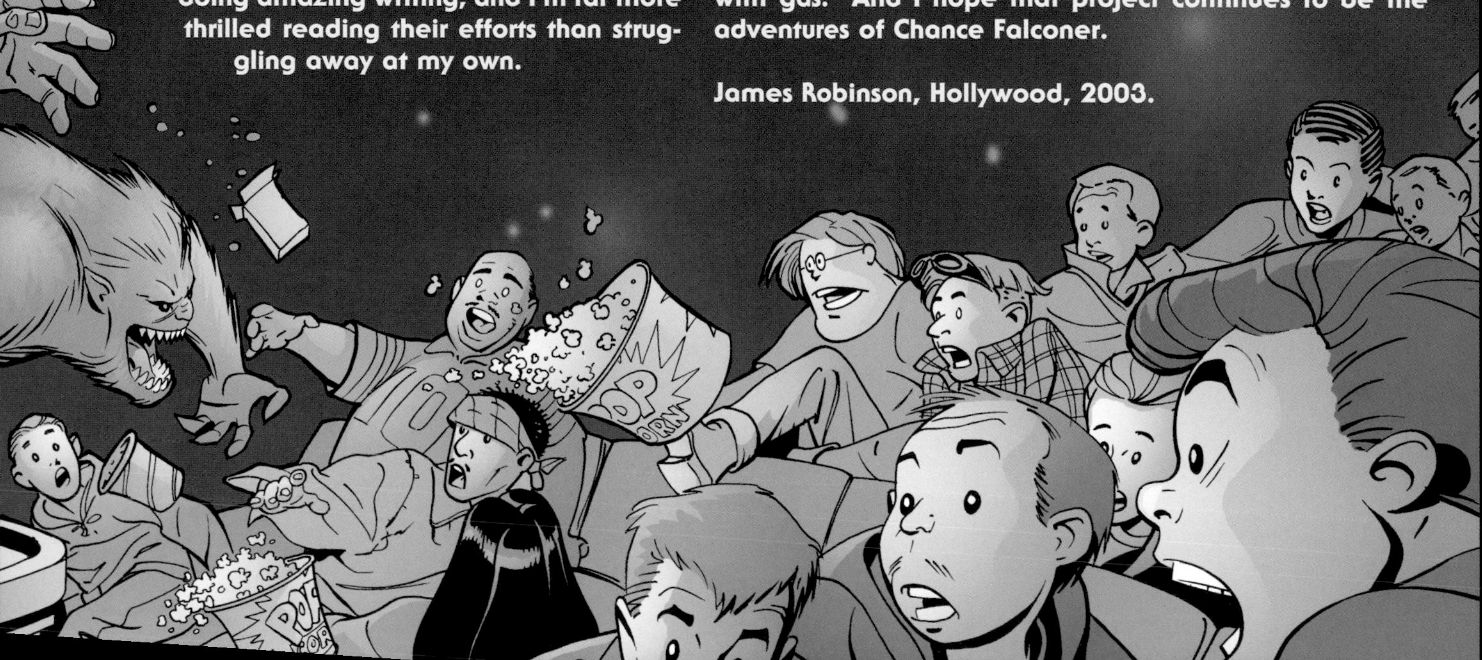
POP
CORN

CHAPTER 1

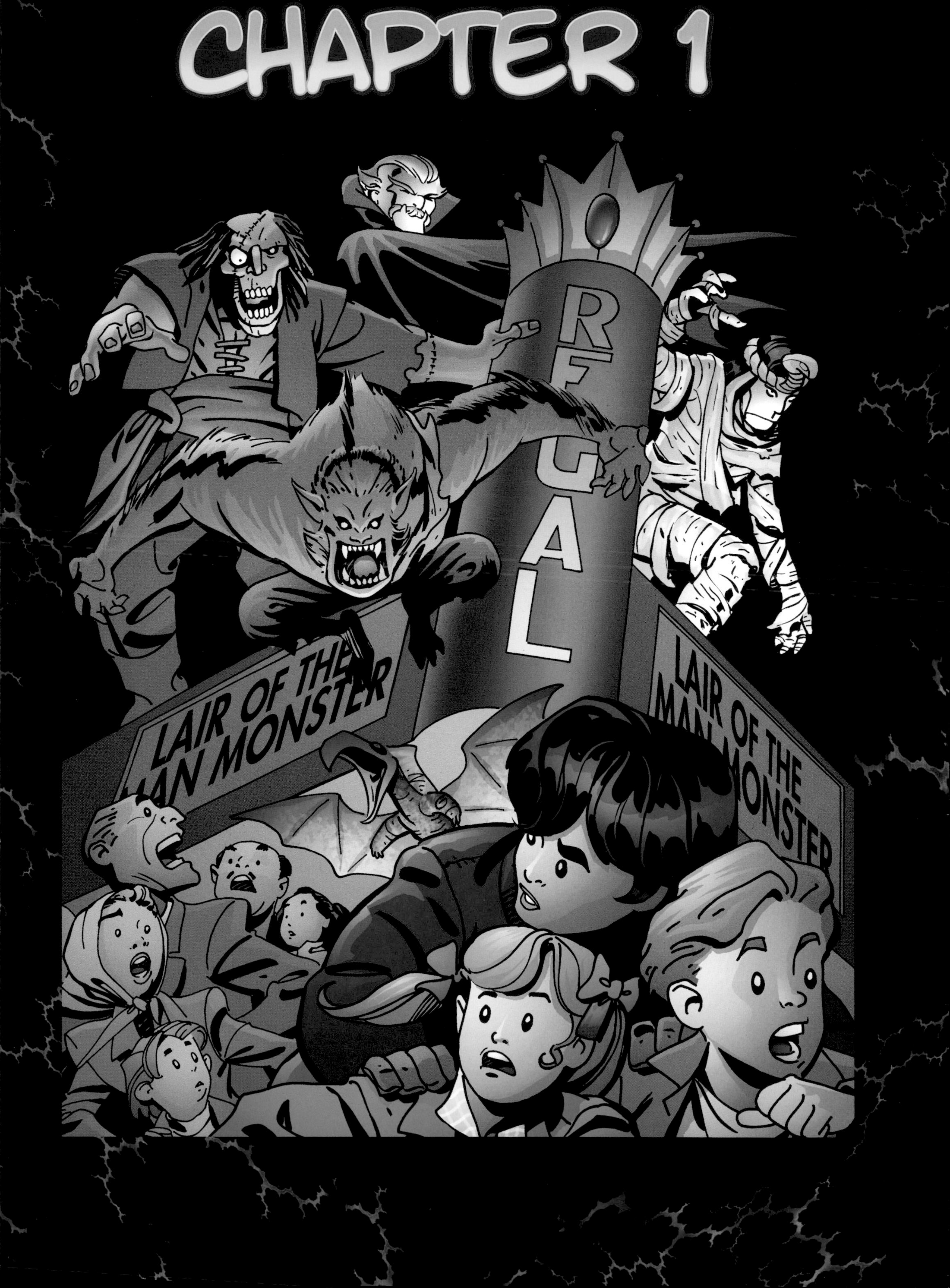
LAIR OF THE MAN MONSTER

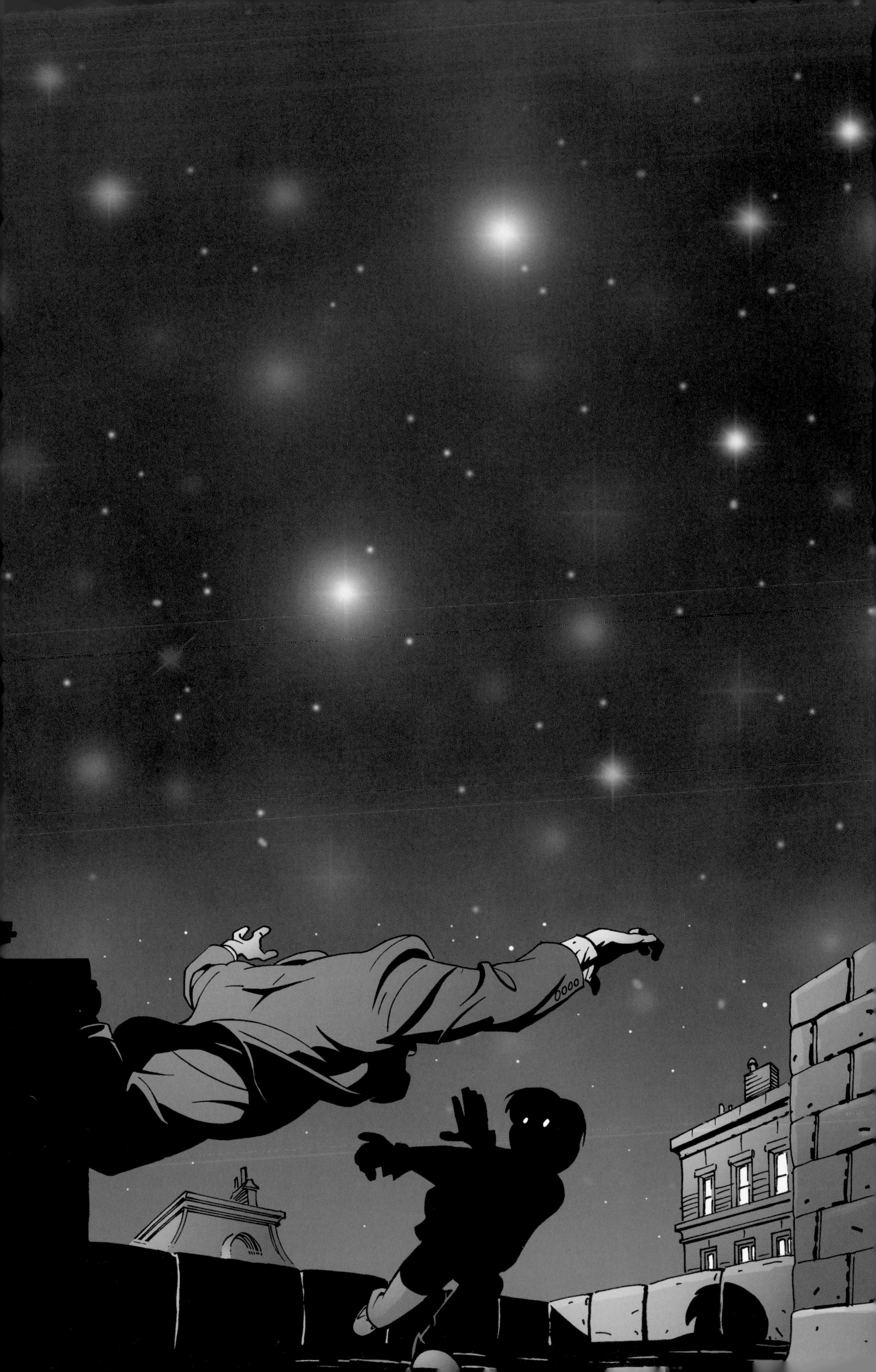

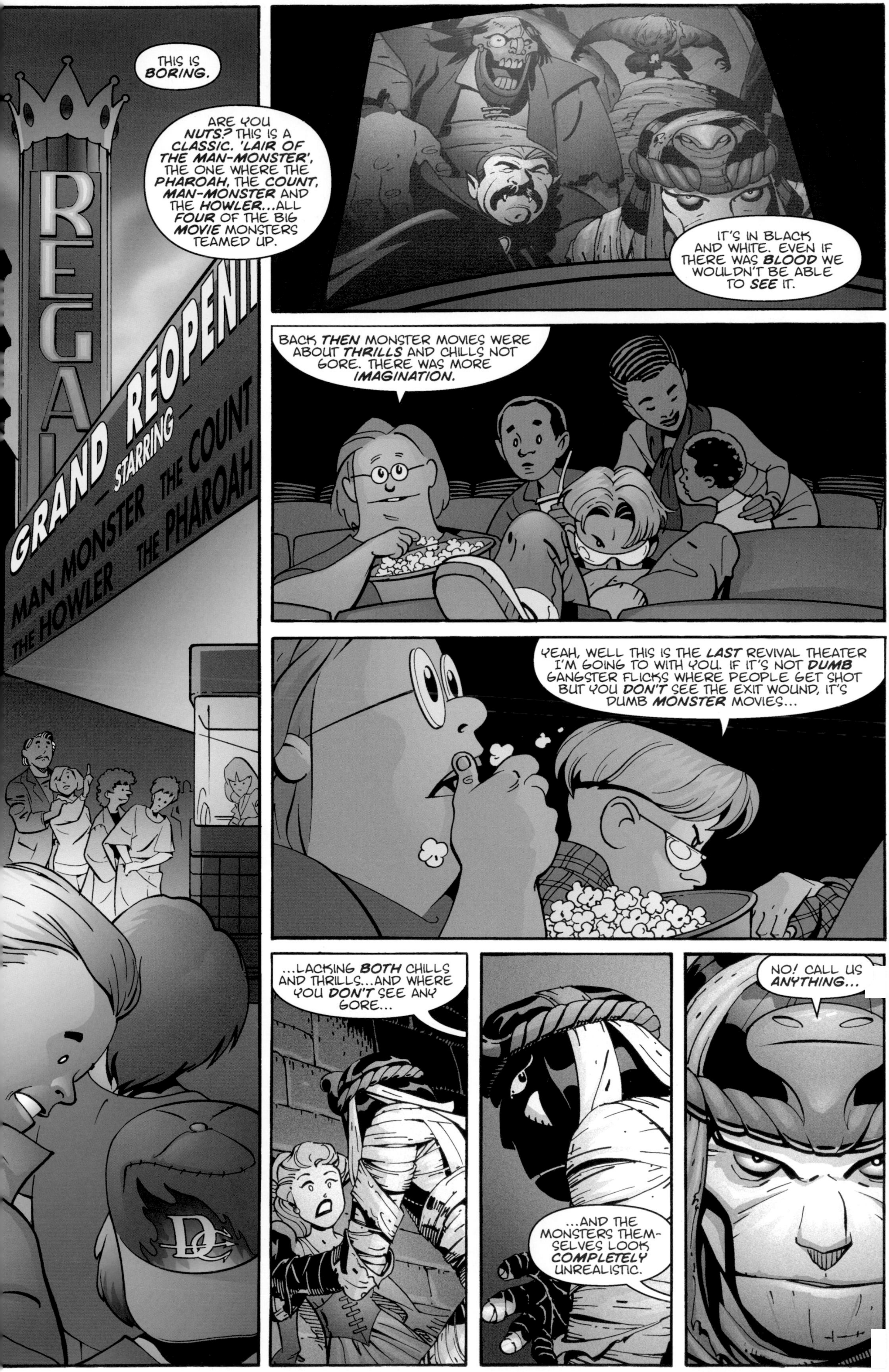
THIS IS BORING.
ARE YOU NUTS? THIS IS A CLASSIC. 'LAIR OF THE MAN-MONSTER', THE ONE WHERE THE PHAROAH, THE COUNT, MAN-MONSTER AND THE HOWLER...ALL FOUR OF THE BIG MOVIE MONSTERS TEAMED UP.
REGAL
GRAND REOPENI
—STARRING—
MAN MONSTER THE COUNT
THE HOWLER THE PHAROAH
IT'S IN BLACK AND WHITE. EVEN IF THERE WAS BLOOD WE WOULDN'T BE ABLE TO SEE IT.
BACK THEN MONSTER MOVIES WERE ABOUT THRILLS AND CHILLS NOT GORE. THERE WAS MORE IMAGINATION.
YEAH, WELL THIS IS THE LAST REVIVAL THEATER I'M GOING TO WITH YOU. IF IT'S NOT DUMB GANGSTER FLICKS WHERE PEOPLE GET SHOT BUT YOU DON'T SEE THE EXIT WOUND, IT'S DUMB MONSTER MOVIES...
...LACKING BOTH CHILLS AND THRILLS...AND WHERE YOU DON'T SEE ANY GORE...
...AND THE MONSTERS THEMSELVES LOOK COMPLETELY UNREALISTIC.
NO! CALL US ANYTHING...

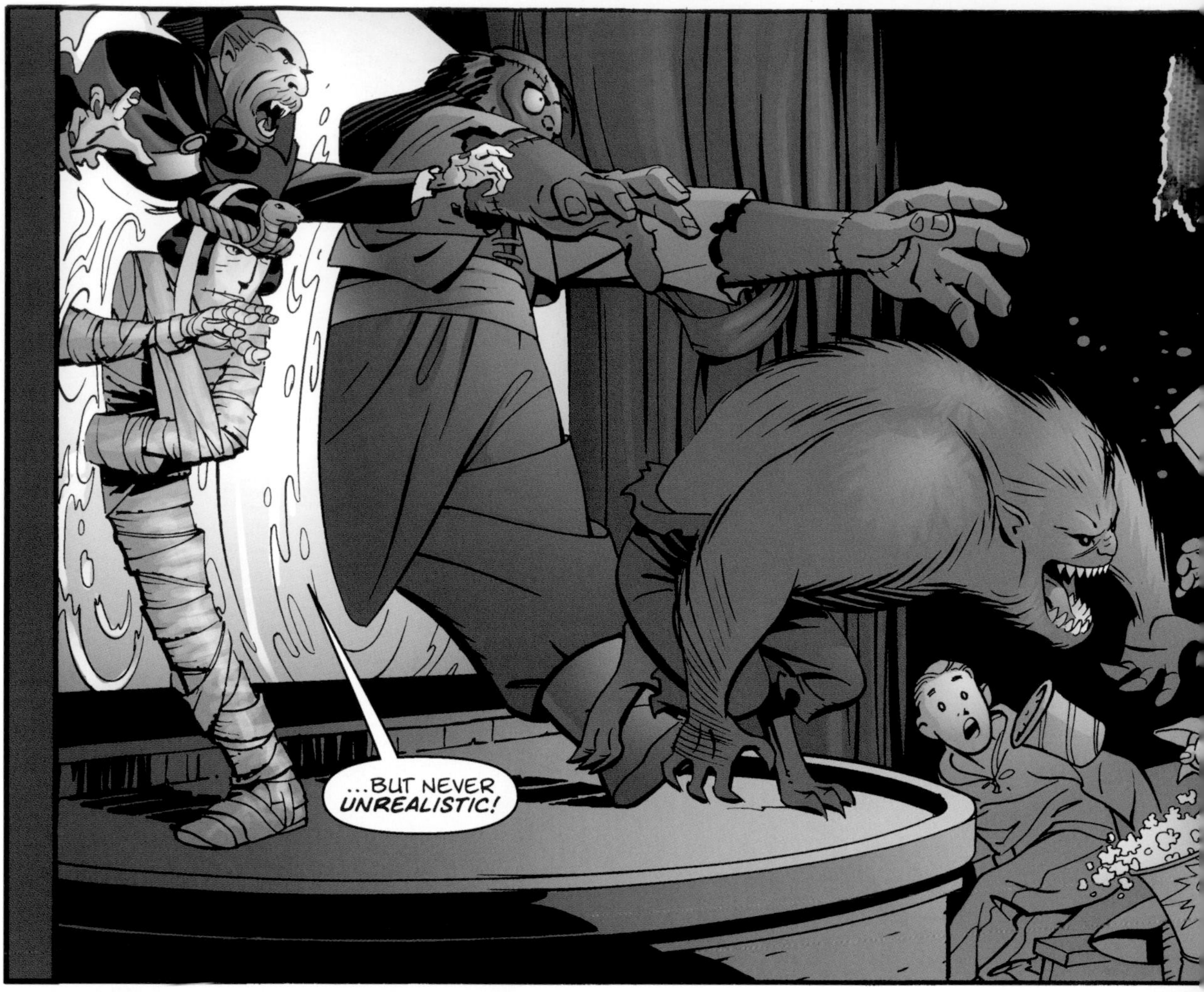
...BUT NEVER UNREALISTIC!

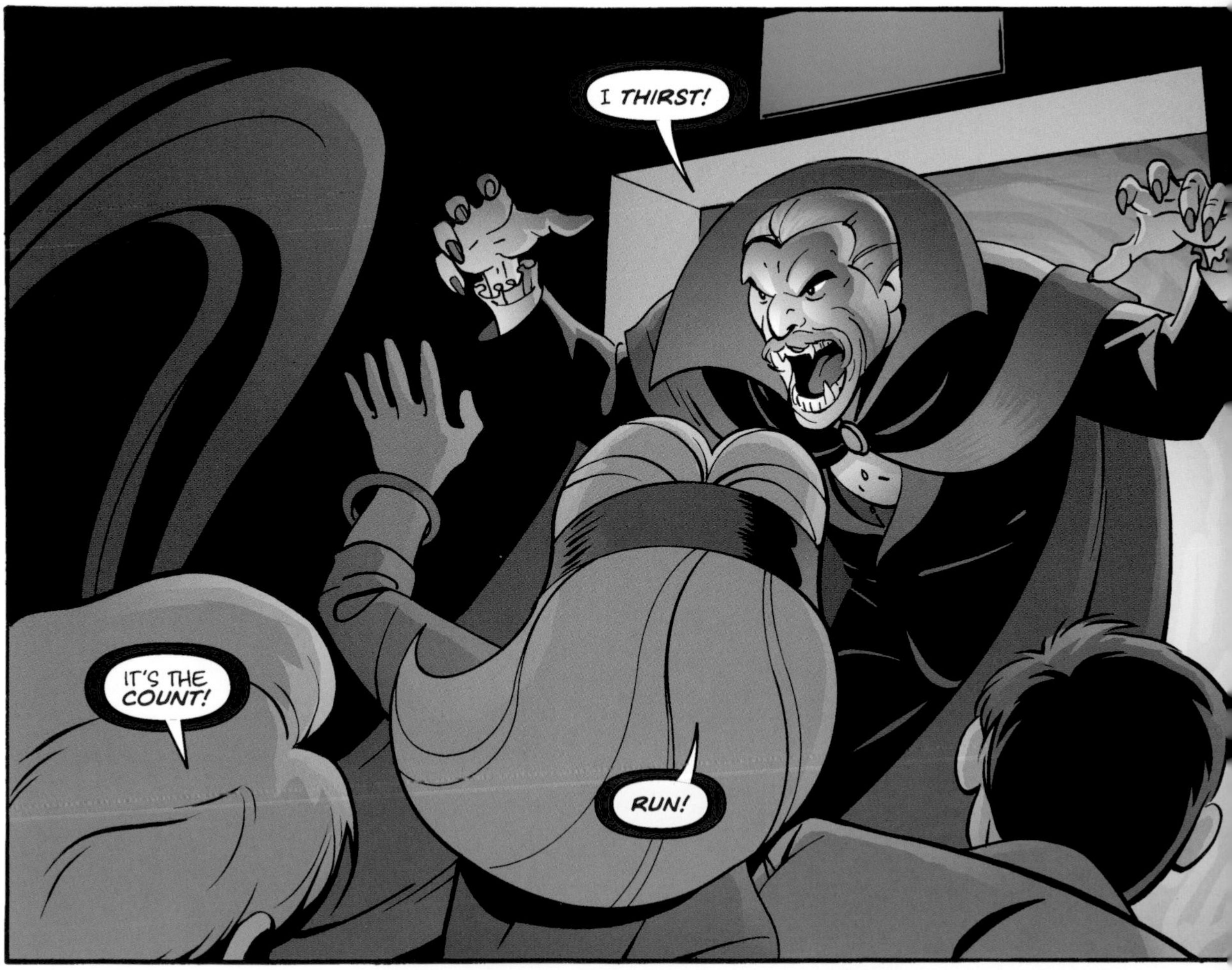
I THIRST!
IT'S THE COUNT!
RUN!

BY JAMES ROBINSON & PAUL SMITH
WITH GEORGE FREEMAN INKS

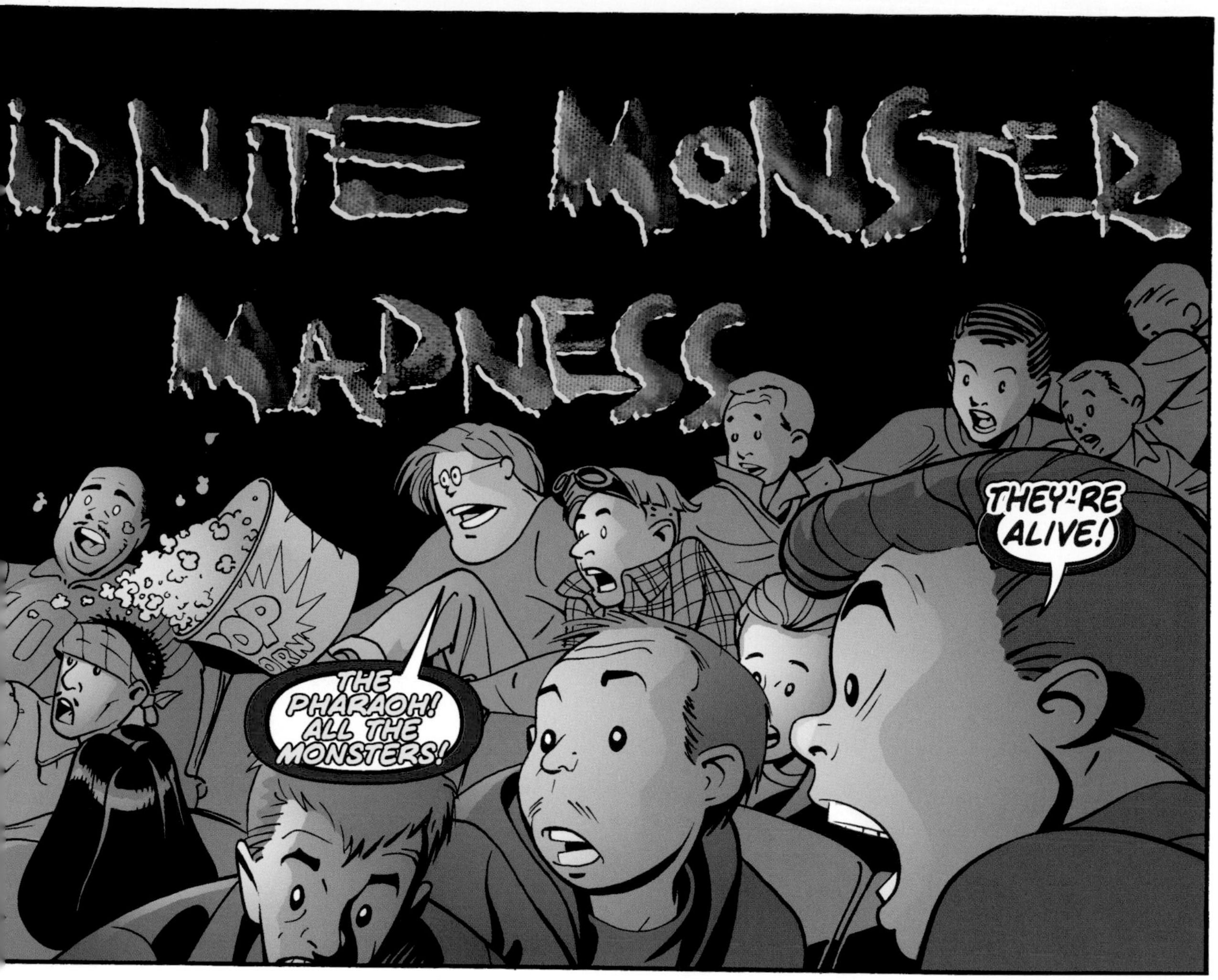

IDNITE MONSTER MADNESS
THE PHARAOH! ALL THE MONSTERS!
THEY'RE ALIVE!

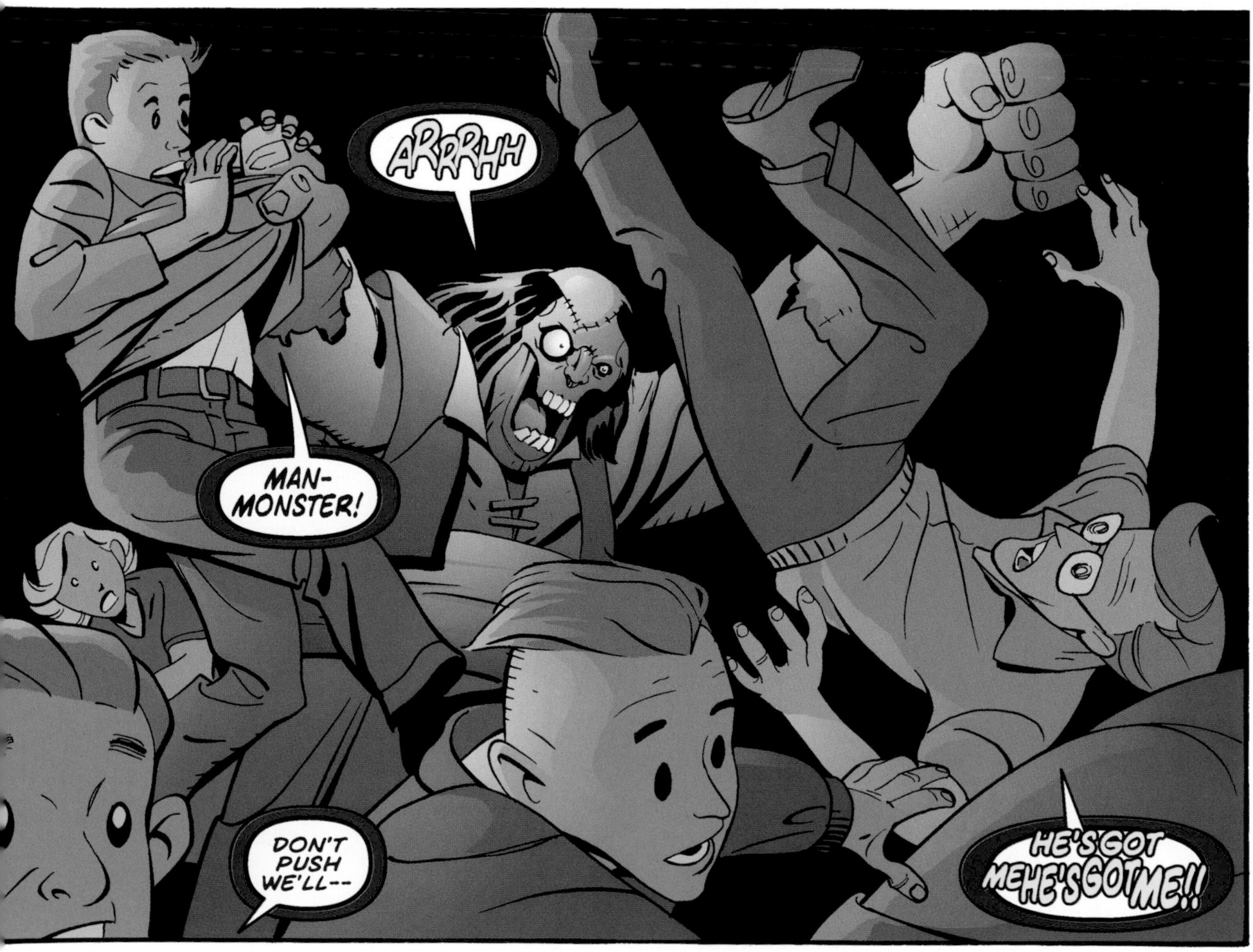

ARRRHH
MAN-MONSTER!
DON'T PUSH WE'LL--
HE'S GOT ME HE'S GOT ME!!

MIE GRENIER LETTERS JEROMY COX COLORS
JONATHAN PETERSON EDITOR

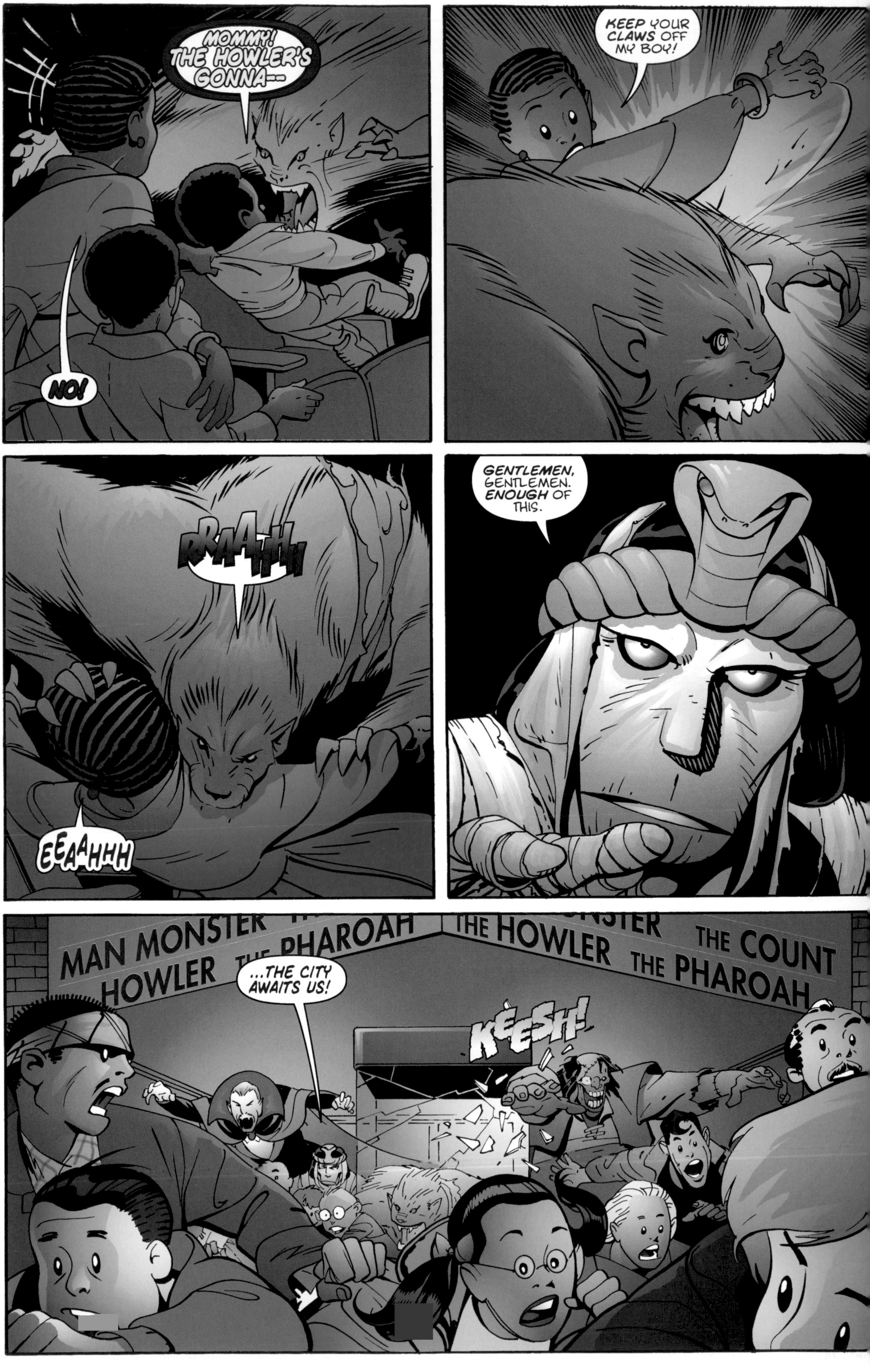
MOMMY! THE HOWLER'S GONNA--
NO!
KEEP YOUR CLAWS OFF MY BOY!
RRAAHHH
EEAAHHH
GENTLEMEN, GENTLEMEN. ENOUGH OF THIS.
MAN MONSTER
HOWLER THE PHAROAH
THE HOWLER THE COUNT
THE PHAROAH
...THE CITY AWAITS US!
KEESH!

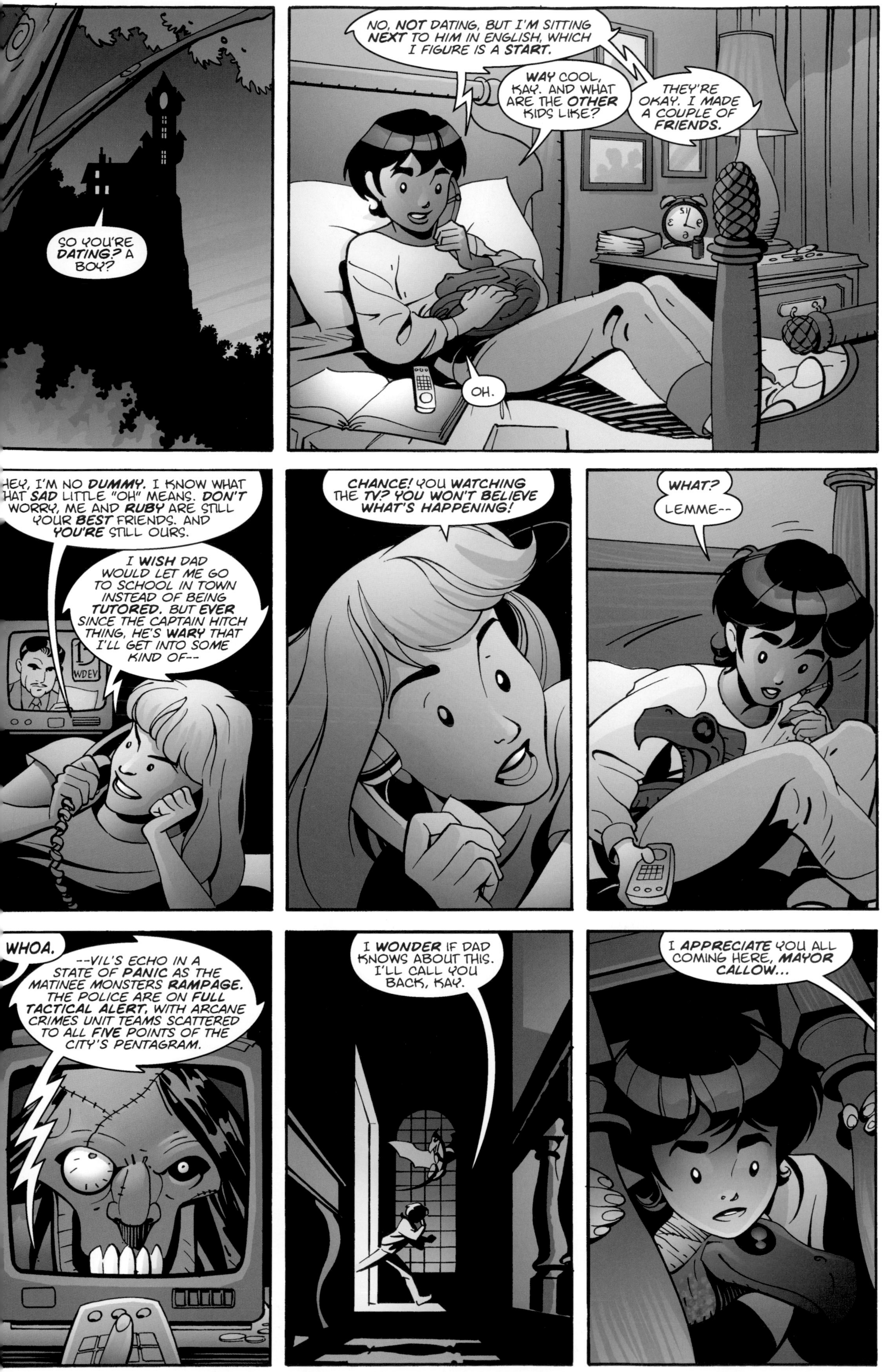
SO YOU'RE DATING? A BOY?
NO, NOT DATING, BUT I'M SITTING NEXT TO HIM IN ENGLISH, WHICH I FIGURE IS A START.
WAY COOL, KAY. AND WHAT ARE THE OTHER KIDS LIKE?
THEY'RE OKAY. I MADE A COUPLE OF FRIENDS.
OH.
HEY, I'M NO DUMMY. I KNOW WHAT THAT SAD LITTLE "OH" MEANS. DON'T WORRY, ME AND RUBY ARE STILL YOUR BEST FRIENDS. AND YOU'RE STILL OURS.
I WISH DAD WOULD LET ME GO TO SCHOOL IN TOWN INSTEAD OF BEING TUTORED. BUT EVER SINCE THE CAPTAIN HITCH THING, HE'S WARY THAT I'LL GET INTO SOME KIND OF--
WDEV
CHANCE! YOU WATCHING THE TV? YOU WON'T BELIEVE WHAT'S HAPPENING!
WHAT?
LEMME--
WHOA.
--VIL'S ECHO IN A STATE OF PANIC AS THE MATINEE MONSTERS RAMPAGE. THE POLICE ARE ON FULL TACTICAL ALERT, WITH ARCANE CRIMES UNIT TEAMS SCATTERED TO ALL FIVE POINTS OF THE CITY'S PENTAGRAM.
I WONDER IF DAD KNOWS ABOUT THIS. I'LL CALL YOU BACK, KAY.
I APPRECIATE YOU ALL COMING HERE, MAYOR CALLOW...

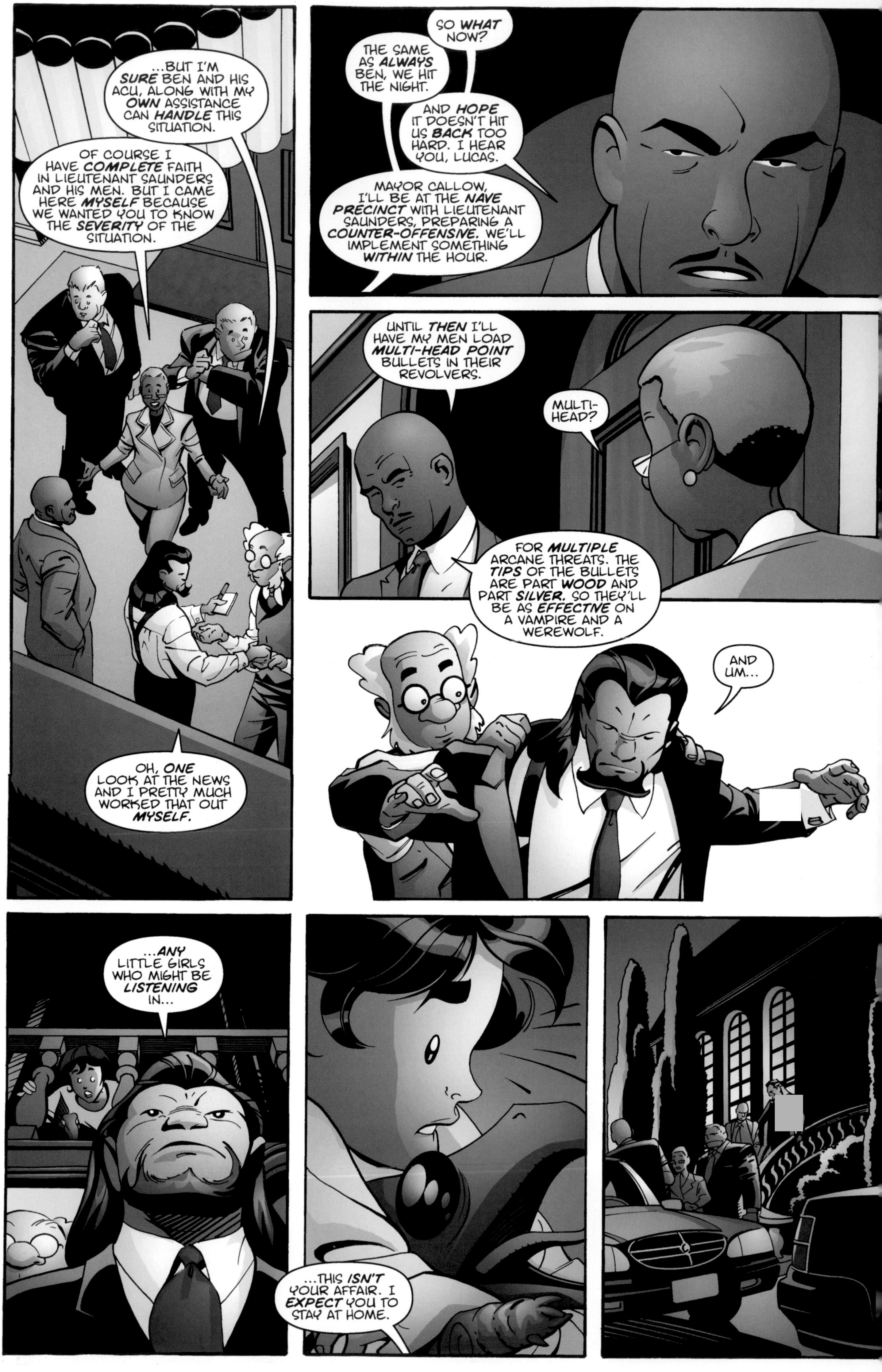

...BUT I'M SURE BEN AND HIS ACU, ALONG WITH MY OWN ASSISTANCE CAN HANDLE THIS SITUATION.
OF COURSE I HAVE COMPLETE FAITH IN LIEUTENANT SAUNDERS AND HIS MEN. BUT I CAME HERE MYSELF BECAUSE WE WANTED YOU TO KNOW THE SEVERITY OF THE SITUATION.
OH, ONE LOOK AT THE NEWS AND I PRETTY MUCH WORKED THAT OUT MYSELF.
SO WHAT NOW?
THE SAME AS ALWAYS BEN, WE HIT THE NIGHT.
AND HOPE IT DOESN'T HIT US BACK TOO HARD. I HEAR YOU, LUCAS.
MAYOR CALLOW, I'LL BE AT THE NAVE PRECINCT WITH LIEUTENANT SAUNDERS, PREPARING A COUNTER-OFFENSIVE. WE'LL IMPLEMENT SOMETHING WITHIN THE HOUR.
UNTIL THEN I'LL HAVE MY MEN LOAD MULTI-HEAD POINT BULLETS IN THEIR REVOLVERS.
MULTI-HEAD?
FOR MULTIPLE ARCANE THREATS. THE TIPS OF THE BULLETS ARE PART WOOD AND PART SILVER. SO THEY'LL BE AS EFFECTIVE ON A VAMPIRE AND A WEREWOLF.
AND UM...
...ANY LITTLE GIRLS WHO MIGHT BE LISTENING IN...
...THIS ISN'T YOUR AFFAIR. I EXPECT YOU TO STAY AT HOME.

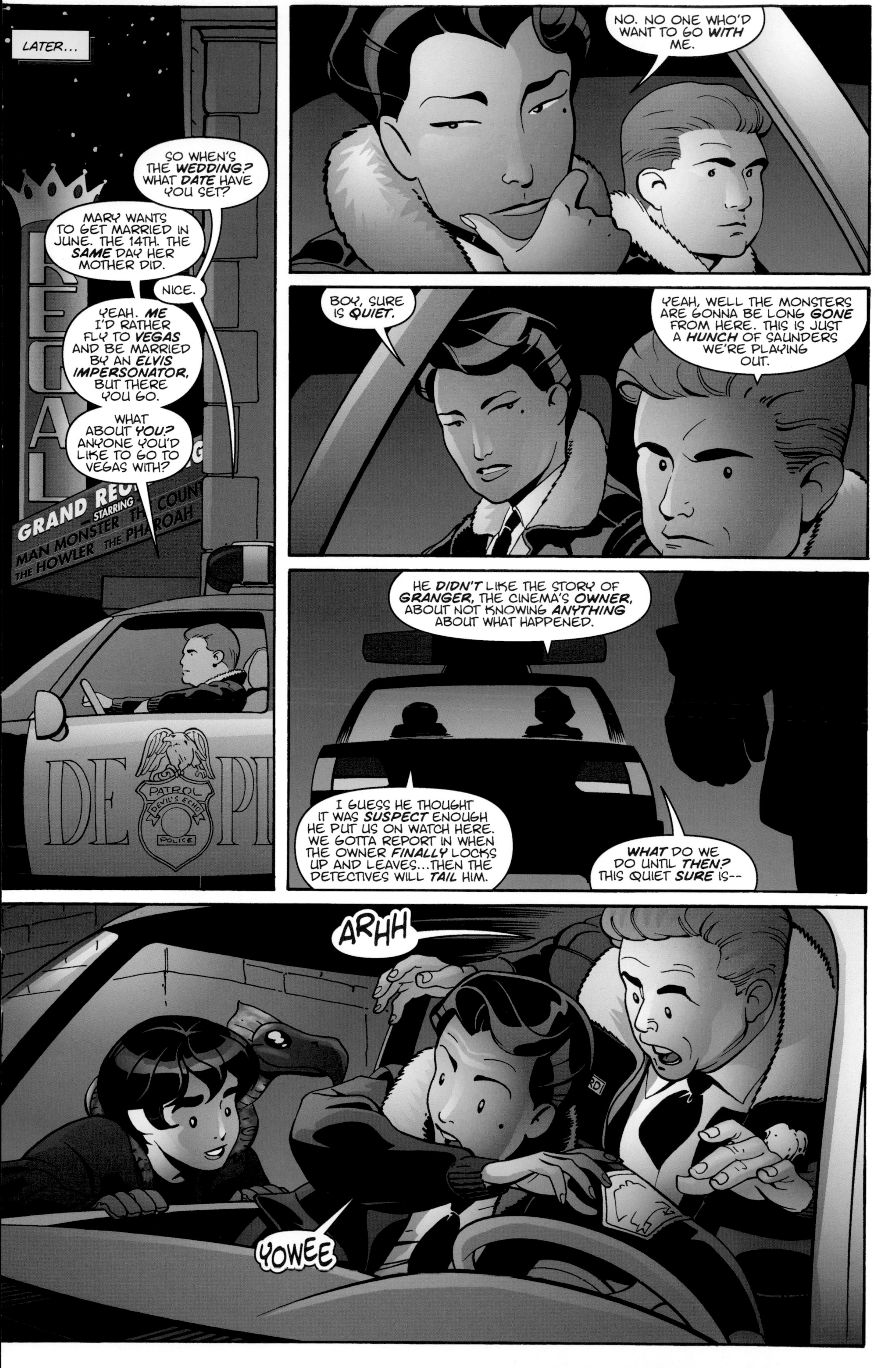
LATER...
SO WHEN'S THE WEDDING? WHAT DATE HAVE YOU SET?
MARY WANTS TO GET MARRIED IN JUNE. THE 14TH. THE SAME DAY HER MOTHER DID.
NICE.
YEAH. ME I'D RATHER FLY TO VEGAS AND BE MARRIED BY AN ELVIS IMPERSONATOR, BUT THERE YOU GO.
WHAT ABOUT YOU? ANYONE YOU'D LIKE TO GO TO VEGAS WITH?
GRAND REO
STARRING
MAN MONSTER THE COUNT
THE HOWLER THE PHAROAH
DE PI
PATROL
DEVIL'S ECHO
POLICE
NO. NO ONE WHO'D WANT TO GO WITH ME.
BOY, SURE IS QUIET.
YEAH, WELL THE MONSTERS ARE GONNA BE LONG GONE FROM HERE. THIS IS JUST A HUNCH OF SAUNDERS WE'RE PLAYING OUT.
HE DIDN'T LIKE THE STORY OF GRANGER, THE CINEMA'S OWNER, ABOUT NOT KNOWING ANYTHING ABOUT WHAT HAPPENED.
I GUESS HE THOUGHT IT WAS SUSPECT ENOUGH HE PUT US ON WATCH HERE. WE GOTTA REPORT IN WHEN THE OWNER FINALLY LOCKS UP AND LEAVES...THEN THE DETECTIVES WILL TAIL HIM.
WHAT DO WE DO UNTIL THEN? THIS QUIET SURE IS--
ARHH
YOWEE

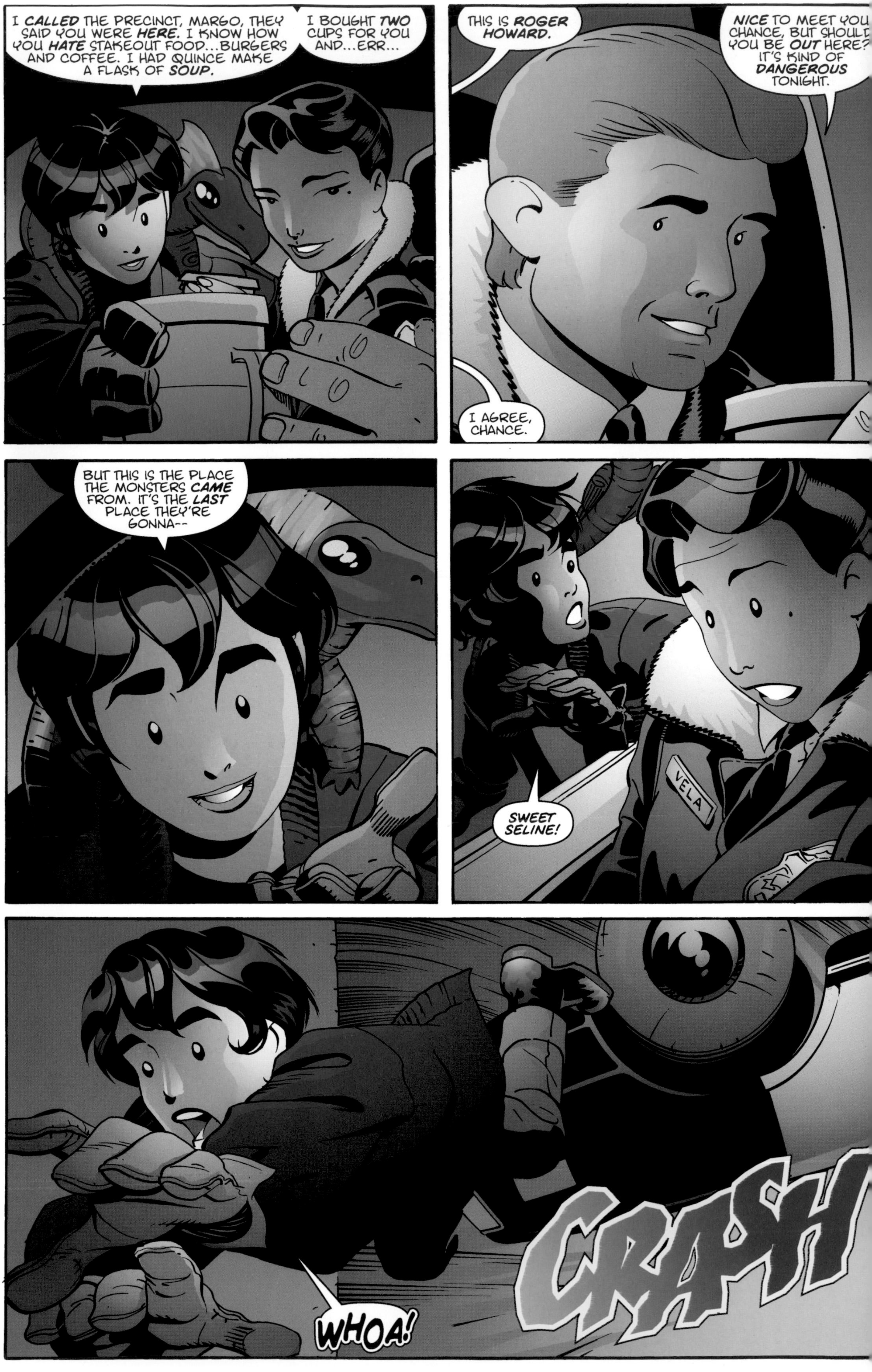
I CALLED THE PRECINCT, MARGO, THEY SAID YOU WERE HERE. I KNOW HOW YOU HATE STAKEOUT FOOD...BURGERS AND COFFEE. I HAD QUINCE MAKE A FLASK OF SOUP.
I BOUGHT TWO CUPS FOR YOU AND...ERR...
THIS IS ROGER HOWARD.
NICE TO MEET YOU CHANCE, BUT SHOULD YOU BE OUT HERE? IT'S KIND OF DANGEROUS TONIGHT.
I AGREE, CHANCE.
BUT THIS IS THE PLACE THE MONSTERS CAME FROM. IT'S THE LAST PLACE THEY'RE GONNA--
VELA
SWEET SELINE!
WHOA!
CRASH

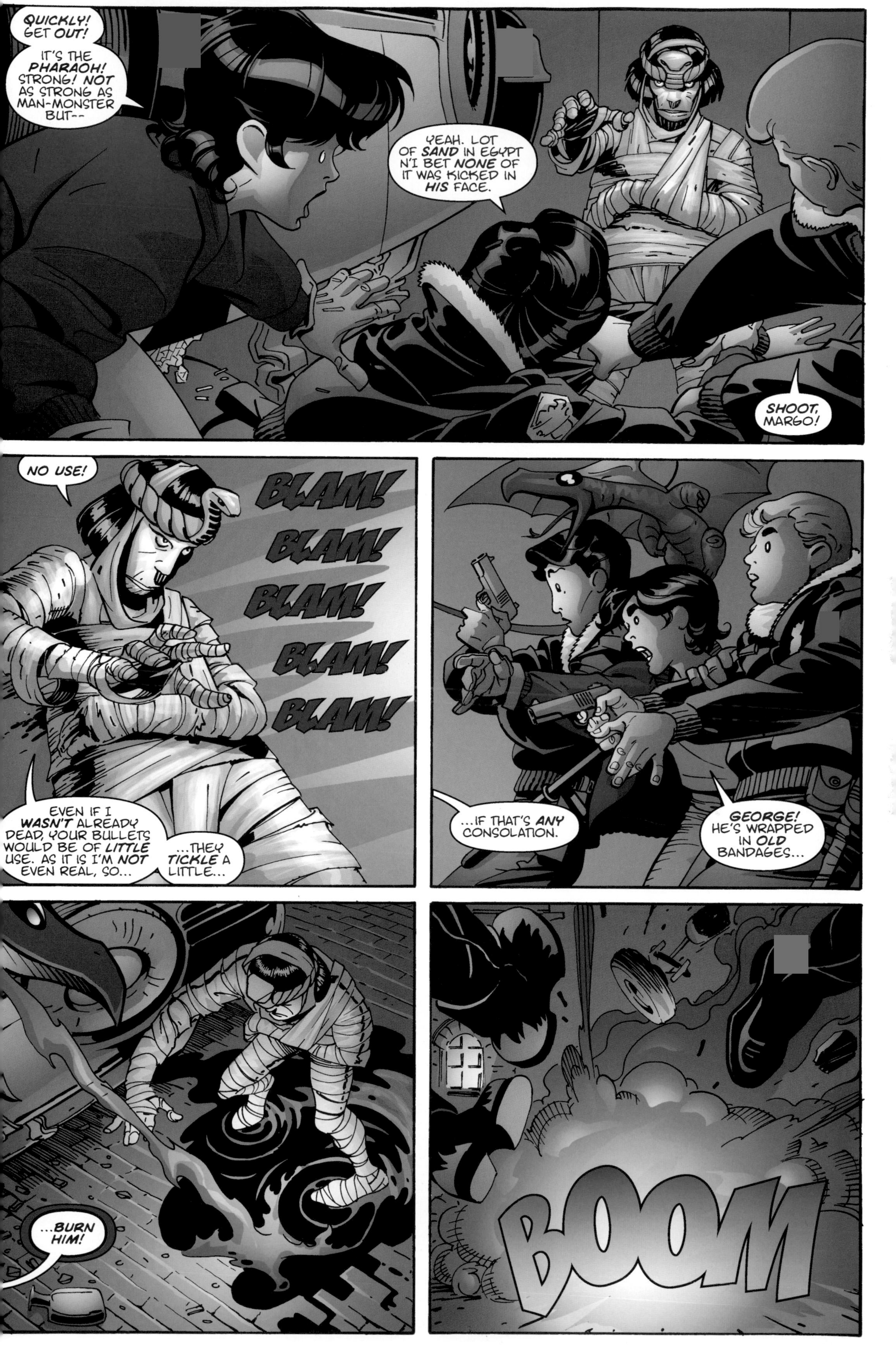
QUICKLY! GET OUT!
IT'S THE PHARAOH! STRONG! NOT AS STRONG AS MAN-MONSTER BUT--
YEAH. LOT OF SAND IN EGYPT N'I BET NONE OF IT WAS KICKED IN HIS FACE.
SHOOT, MARGO!
NO USE!
BLAM!
BLAM!
BLAM!
BLAM!
BLAM!
EVEN IF I WASN'T ALREADY DEAD, YOUR BULLETS WOULD BE OF LITTLE USE. AS IT IS I'M NOT EVEN REAL, SO...
...THEY TICKLE A LITTLE...
...IF THAT'S ANY CONSOLATION.
GEORGE! HE'S WRAPPED IN OLD BANDAGES...
...BURN HIM!
BOOM

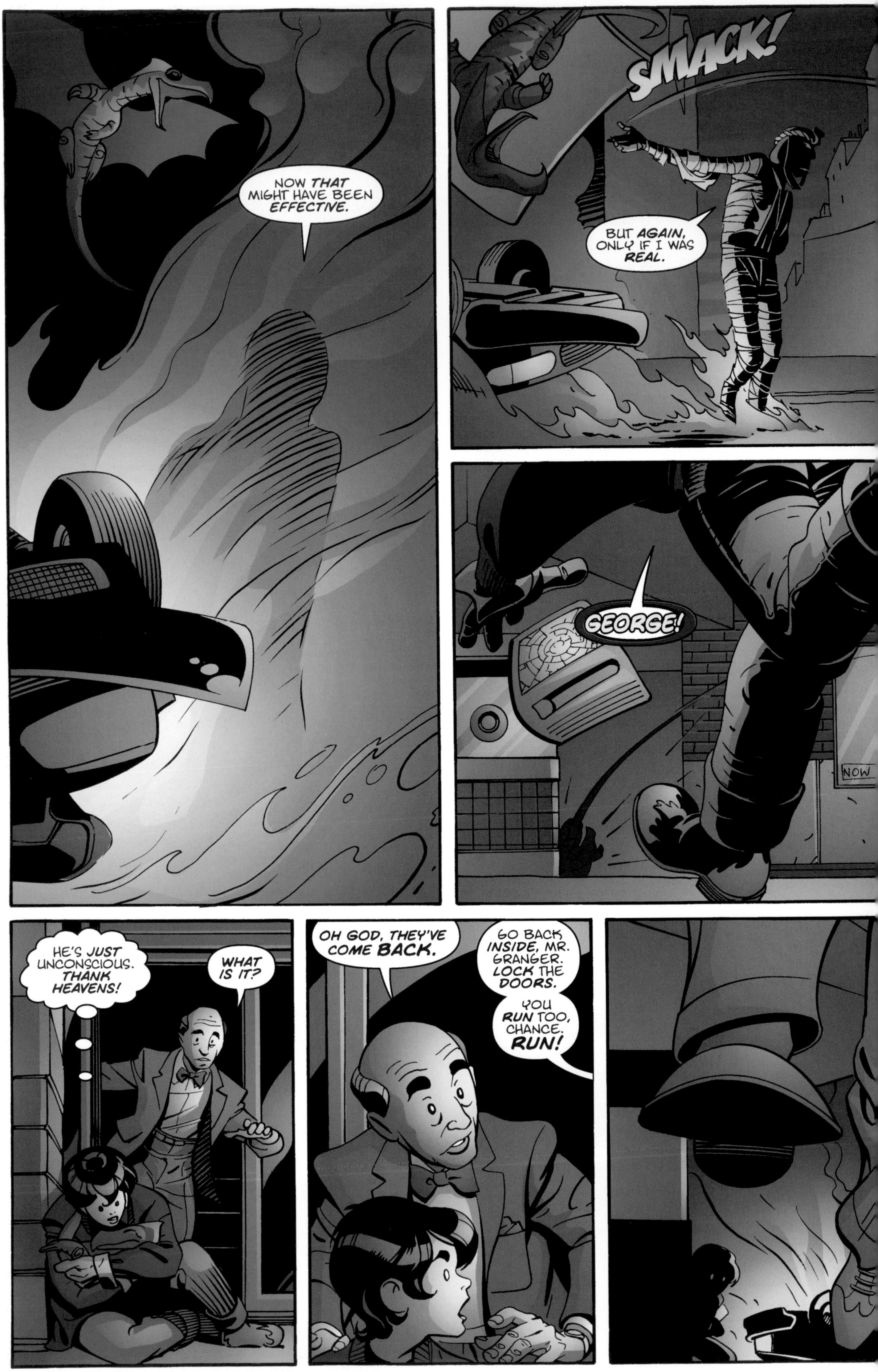
NOW THAT MIGHT HAVE BEEN EFFECTIVE.
SMACK!
BUT AGAIN, ONLY IF I WAS REAL.
GEORGE!
NOW
HE'S JUST UNCONSCIOUS. THANK HEAVENS!
WHAT IS IT?
OH GOD, THEY'VE COME BACK.
GO BACK INSIDE, MR. GRANGER. LOCK THE DOORS.
YOU RUN TOO, CHANCE. RUN!

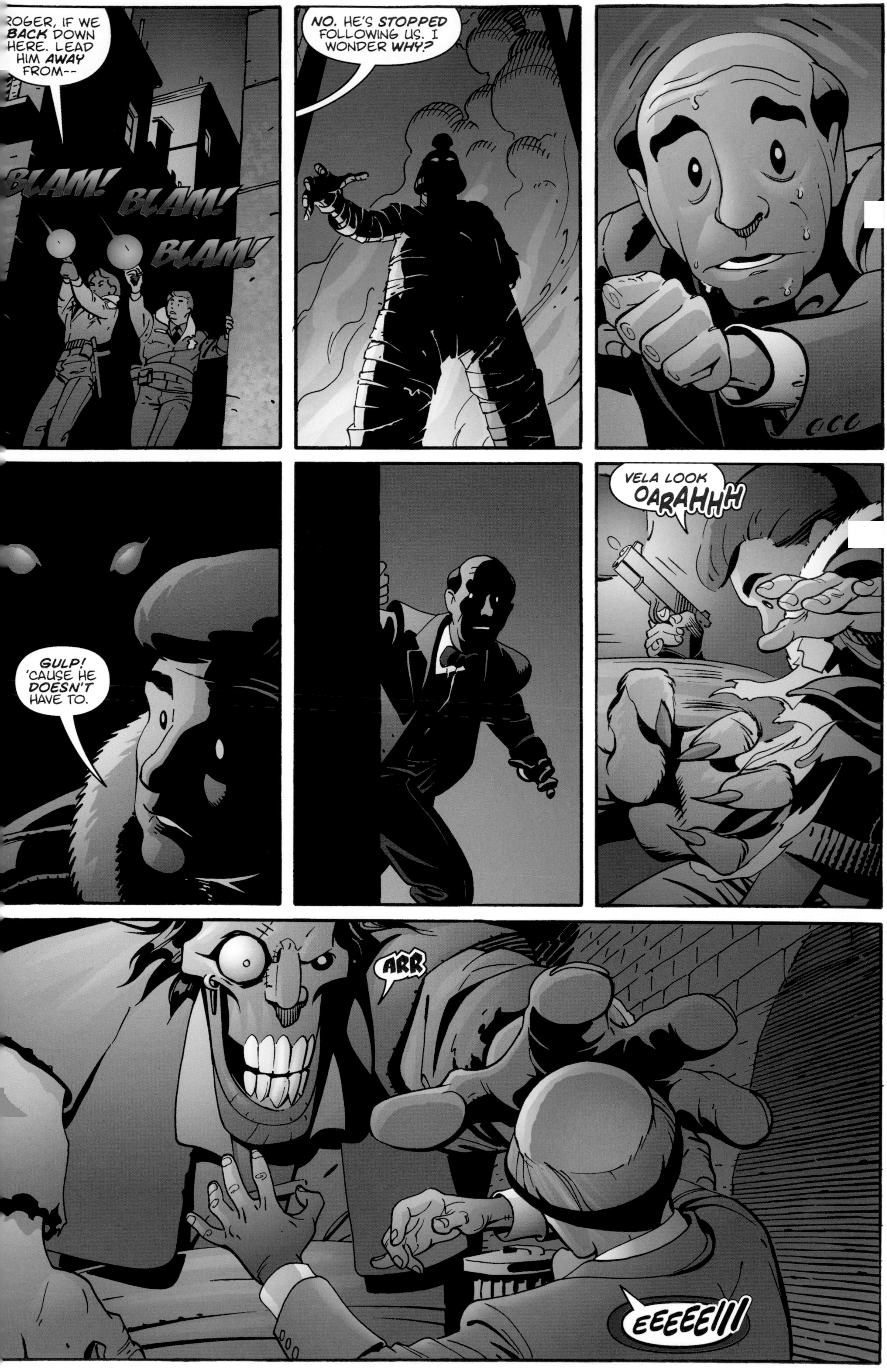
ROGER, IF WE BACK DOWN HERE. LEAD HIM AWAY FROM--
BLAM! BLAM! BLAM!
NO. HE'S STOPPED FOLLOWING US. I WONDER WHY?
GULP! 'CAUSE HE DOESN'T HAVE TO.
VELA LOOK OARAHHH
ARR
EEEEE!!!

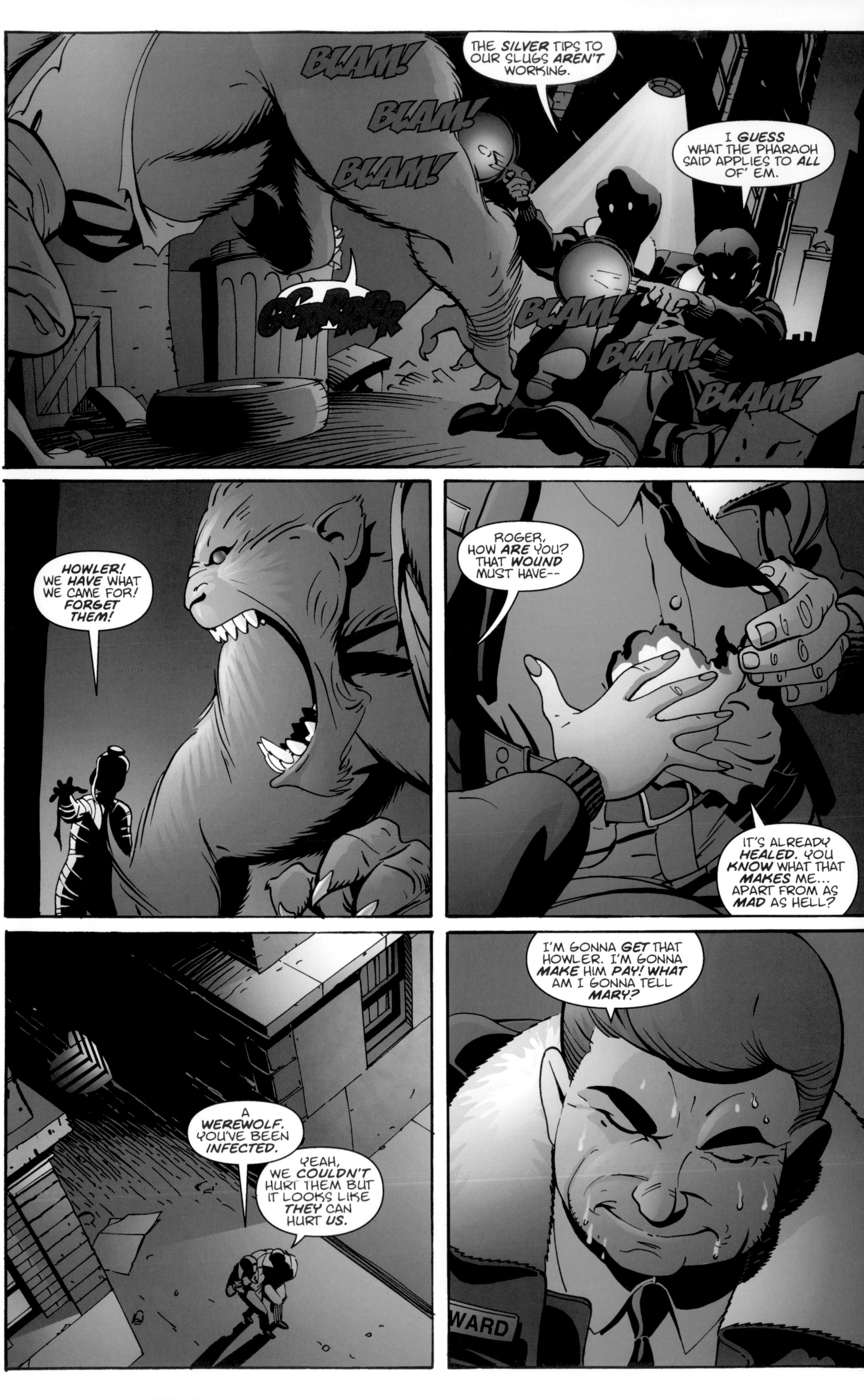

BLAM!
BLAM!
BLAM!
THE SILVER TIPS TO OUR SLUGS AREN'T WORKING.
I GUESS WHAT THE PHARAOH SAID APPLIES TO ALL OF' EM.
BLAM!
BLAM!
BLAM!
HOWLER! WE HAVE WHAT WE CAME FOR! FORGET THEM!
ROGER, HOW ARE YOU? THAT WOUND MUST HAVE--
IT'S ALREADY HEALED. YOU KNOW WHAT THAT MAKES ME... APART FROM AS MAD AS HELL?
A WEREWOLF. YOU'VE BEEN INFECTED.
YEAH, WE COULDN'T HURT THEM BUT IT LOOKS LIKE THEY CAN HURT US.
I'M GONNA GET THAT HOWLER. I'M GONNA MAKE HIM PAY! WHAT AM I GONNA TELL MARY?
WARD

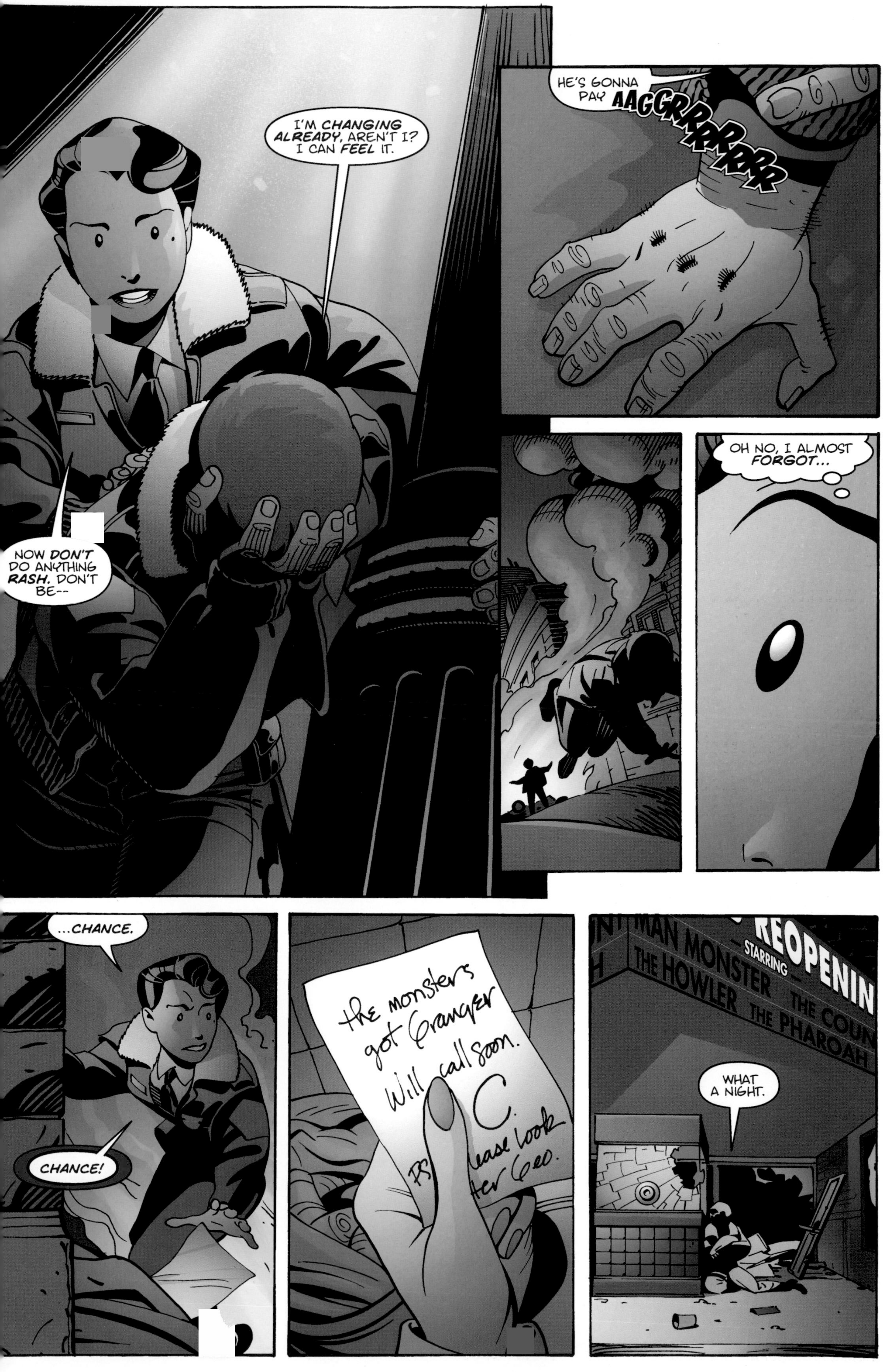

I'M CHANGING ALREADY, AREN'T I? I CAN FEEL IT.
NOW DON'T DO ANYTHING RASH. DON'T BE--
HE'S GONNA PAY AAGGRRRRRRRRR
OH NO, I ALMOST FORGOT...
...CHANCE.
CHANCE!
the monsters got Granger Will call soon.
C.
STARRING
MAN MONSTER
THE HOWLER
THE PHAROAH
WHAT A NIGHT.

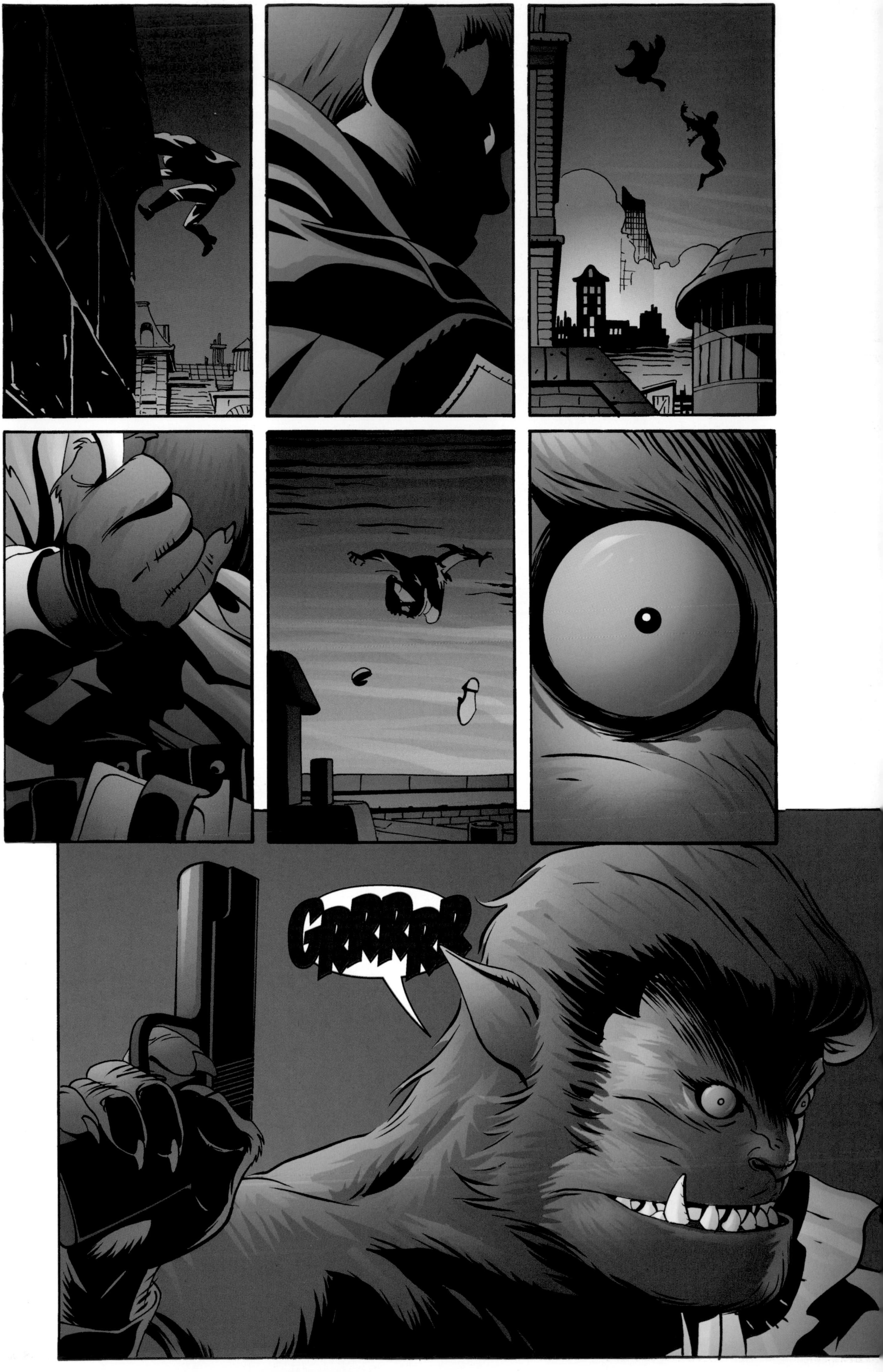
GRRRRR

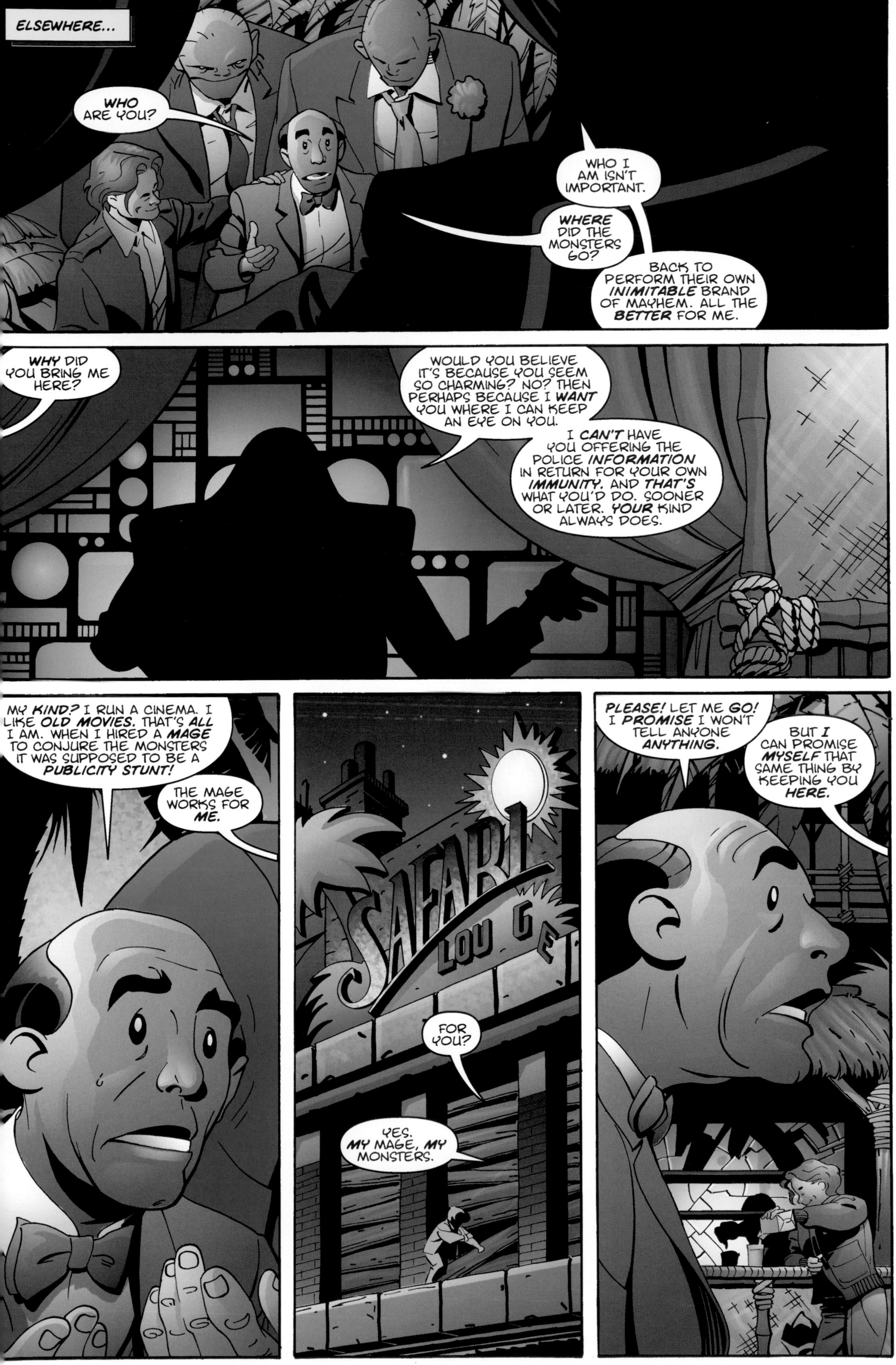
ELSEWHERE...
WHO ARE YOU?
WHO I AM ISN'T IMPORTANT.
WHERE DID THE MONSTERS GO?
BACK TO PERFORM THEIR OWN INIMITABLE BRAND OF MAYHEM. ALL THE BETTER FOR ME.
WHY DID YOU BRING ME HERE?
WOULD YOU BELIEVE IT'S BECAUSE YOU SEEM SO CHARMING? NO? THEN PERHAPS BECAUSE I WANT YOU WHERE I CAN KEEP AN EYE ON YOU.
I CAN'T HAVE YOU OFFERING THE POLICE INFORMATION IN RETURN FOR YOUR OWN IMMUNITY. AND THAT'S WHAT YOU'D DO. SOONER OR LATER. YOUR KIND ALWAYS DOES.
MY KIND? I RUN A CINEMA. I LIKE OLD MOVIES. THAT'S ALL I AM. WHEN I HIRED A MAGE TO CONJURE THE MONSTERS IT WAS SUPPOSED TO BE A PUBLICITY STUNT!
THE MAGE WORKS FOR ME.
SAFARI LOU GE
FOR YOU?
YES. MY MAGE, MY MONSTERS.
PLEASE! LET ME GO! I PROMISE I WON'T TELL ANYONE ANYTHING.
BUT I CAN PROMISE MYSELF THAT SAME THING BY KEEPING YOU HERE.

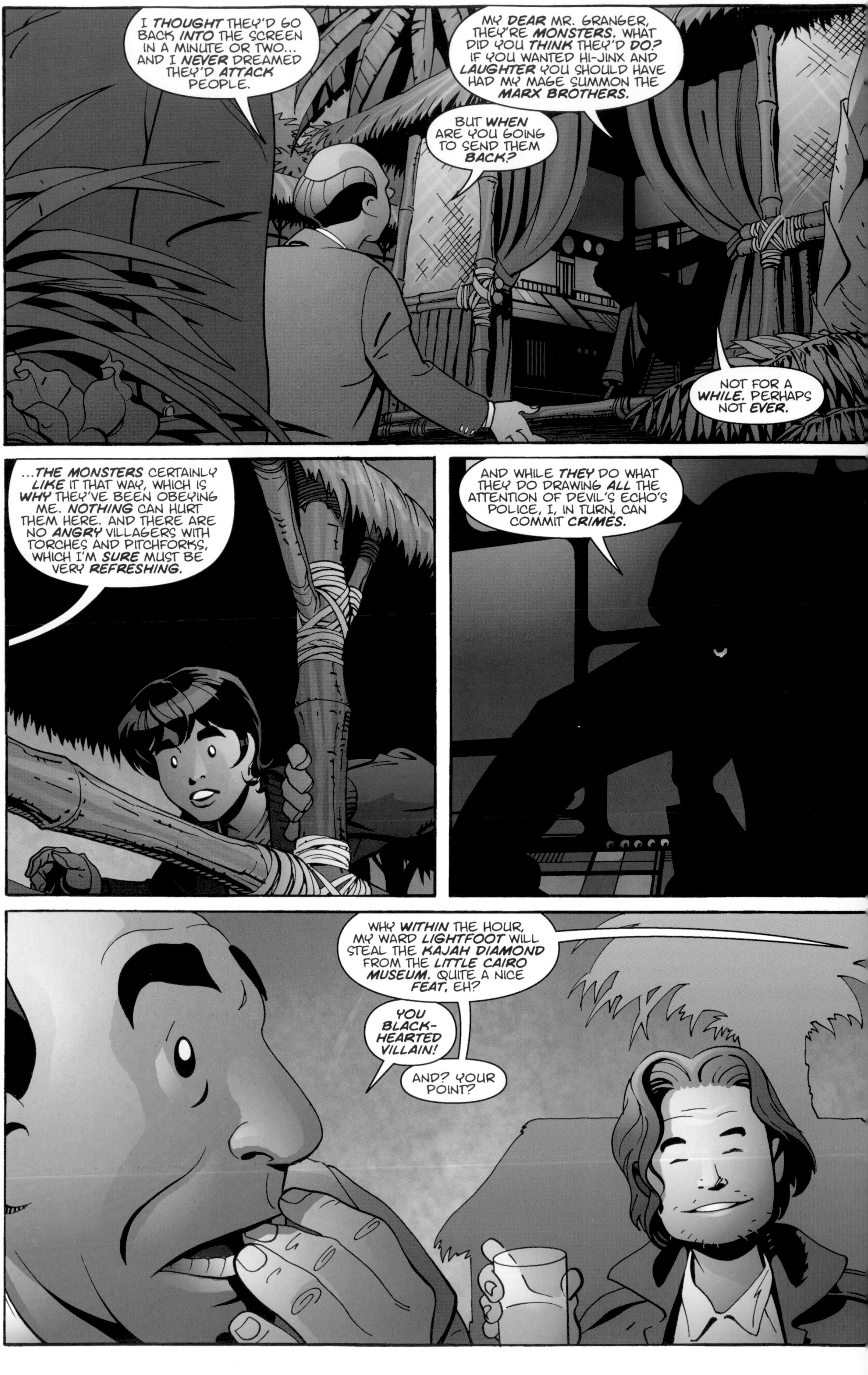
I THOUGHT THEY'D GO BACK INTO THE SCREEN IN A MINUTE OR TWO... AND I NEVER DREAMED THEY'D ATTACK PEOPLE.
MY DEAR MR. GRANGER, THEY'RE MONSTERS. WHAT DID YOU THINK THEY'D DO? IF YOU WANTED HI-JINX AND LAUGHTER YOU SHOULD HAVE HAD MY MAGE SUMMON THE MARX BROTHERS.
BUT WHEN ARE YOU GOING TO SEND THEM BACK?
NOT FOR A WHILE. PERHAPS NOT EVER.
...THE MONSTERS CERTAINLY LIKE IT THAT WAY, WHICH IS WHY THEY'VE BEEN OBEYING ME. NOTHING CAN HURT THEM HERE. AND THERE ARE NO ANGRY VILLAGERS WITH TORCHES AND PITCHFORKS, WHICH I'M SURE MUST BE VERY REFRESHING.
AND WHILE THEY DO WHAT THEY DO DRAWING ALL THE ATTENTION OF DEVIL'S ECHO'S POLICE, I, IN TURN, CAN COMMIT CRIMES.
WHY WITHIN THE HOUR, MY WARD LIGHTFOOT WILL STEAL THE KAJAH DIAMOND FROM THE LITTLE CAIRO MUSEUM. QUITE A NICE FEAT, EH?
YOU BLACK-HEARTED VILLAIN!
AND? YOUR POINT?

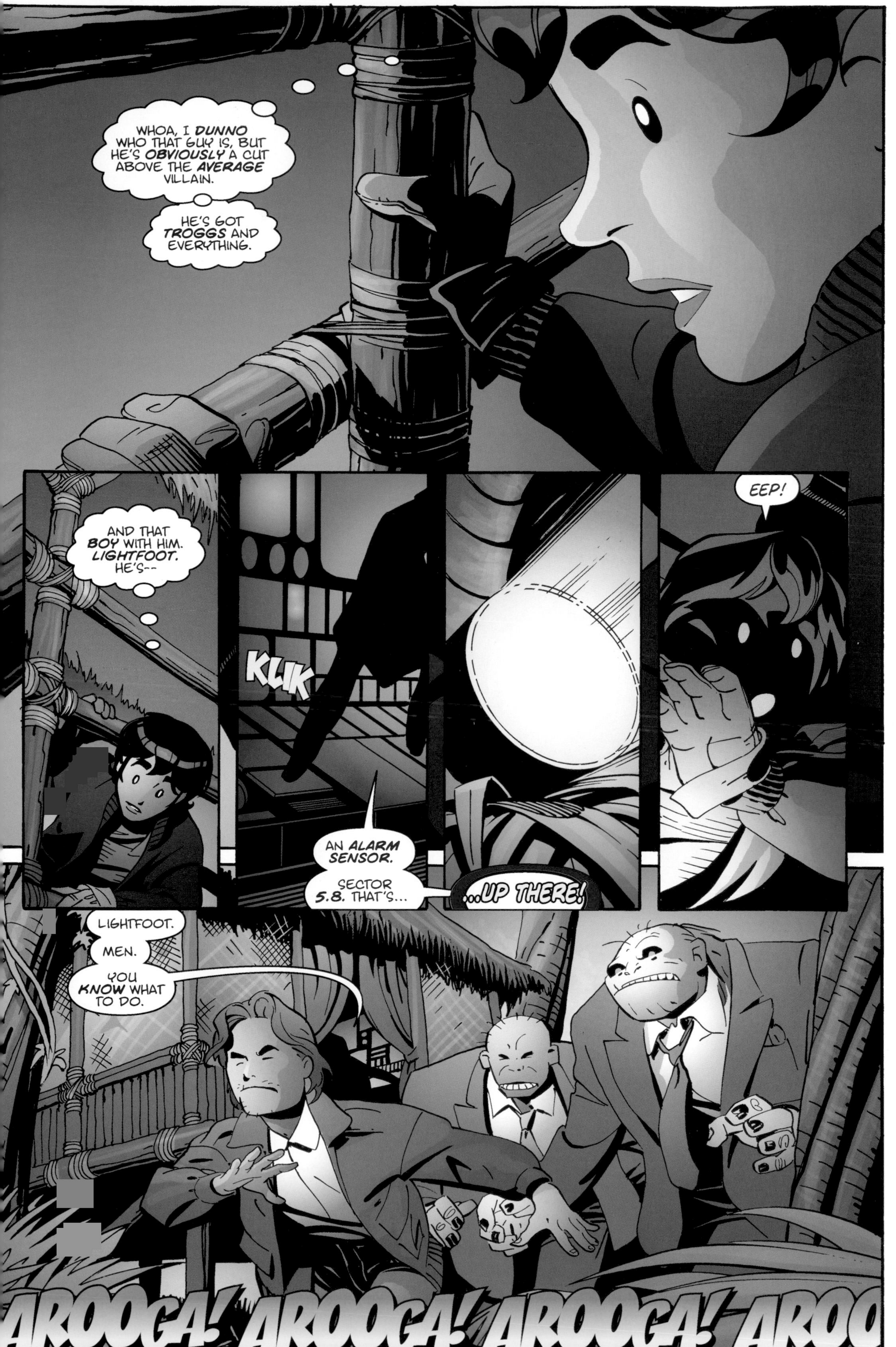
WHOA, I DUNNO WHO THAT GUY IS, BUT HE'S OBVIOUSLY A CUT ABOVE THE AVERAGE VILLAIN.
HE'S GOT TROGGS AND EVERYTHING.
AND THAT BOY WITH HIM. LIGHTFOOT. HE'S--
KLIK
AN ALARM SENSOR.
SECTOR 5.8. THAT'S...
...UP THERE!
EEP!
LIGHTFOOT.
MEN.
YOU KNOW WHAT TO DO.
AROOGA! AROOGA! AROOGA! AROO

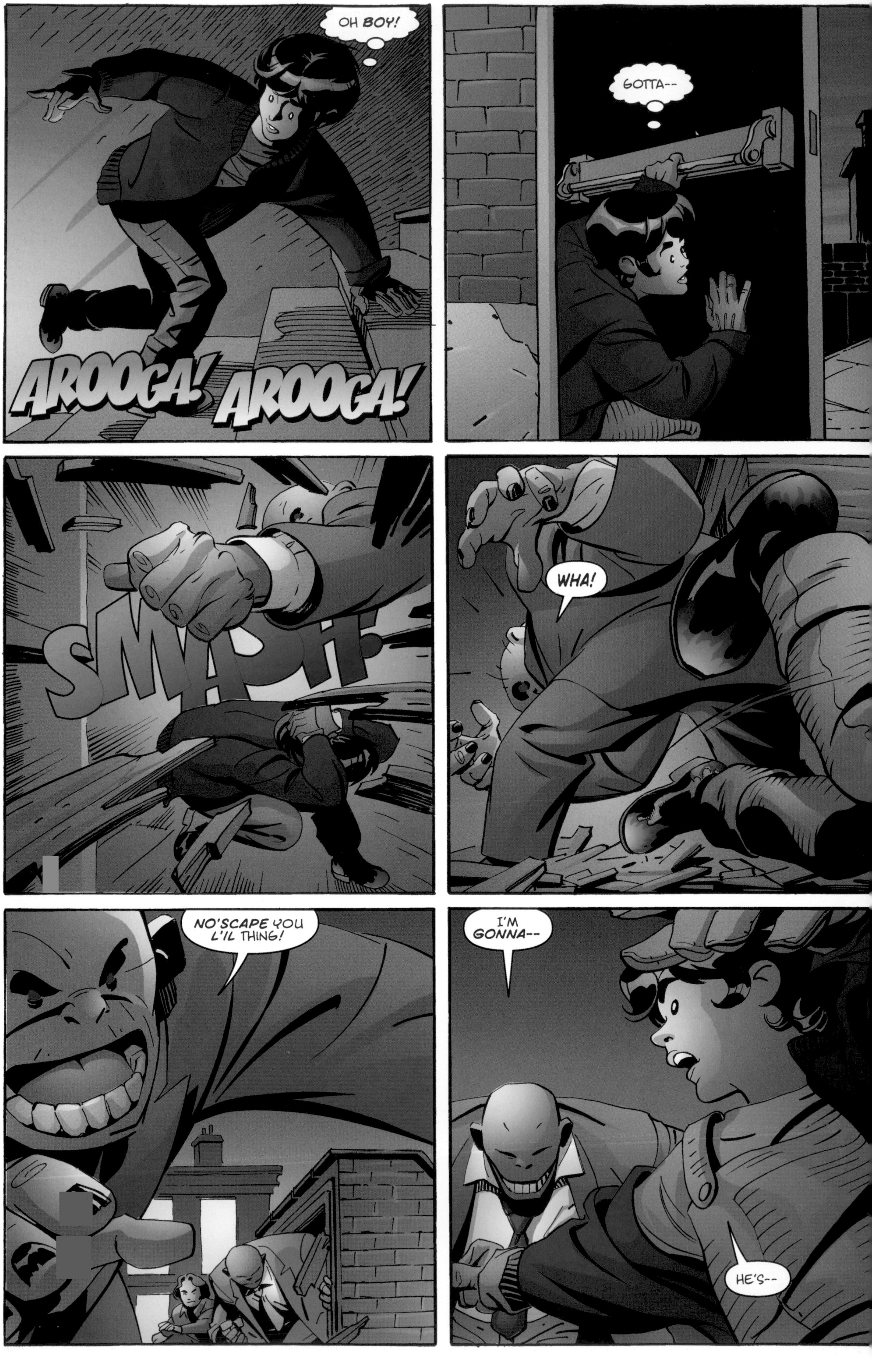

OH BOY!
AROOGA! AROOGA!
GOTTA--
SMASH!
WHA!
NO'SCAPE YOU L'IL THING!
I'M GONNA--
HE'S--

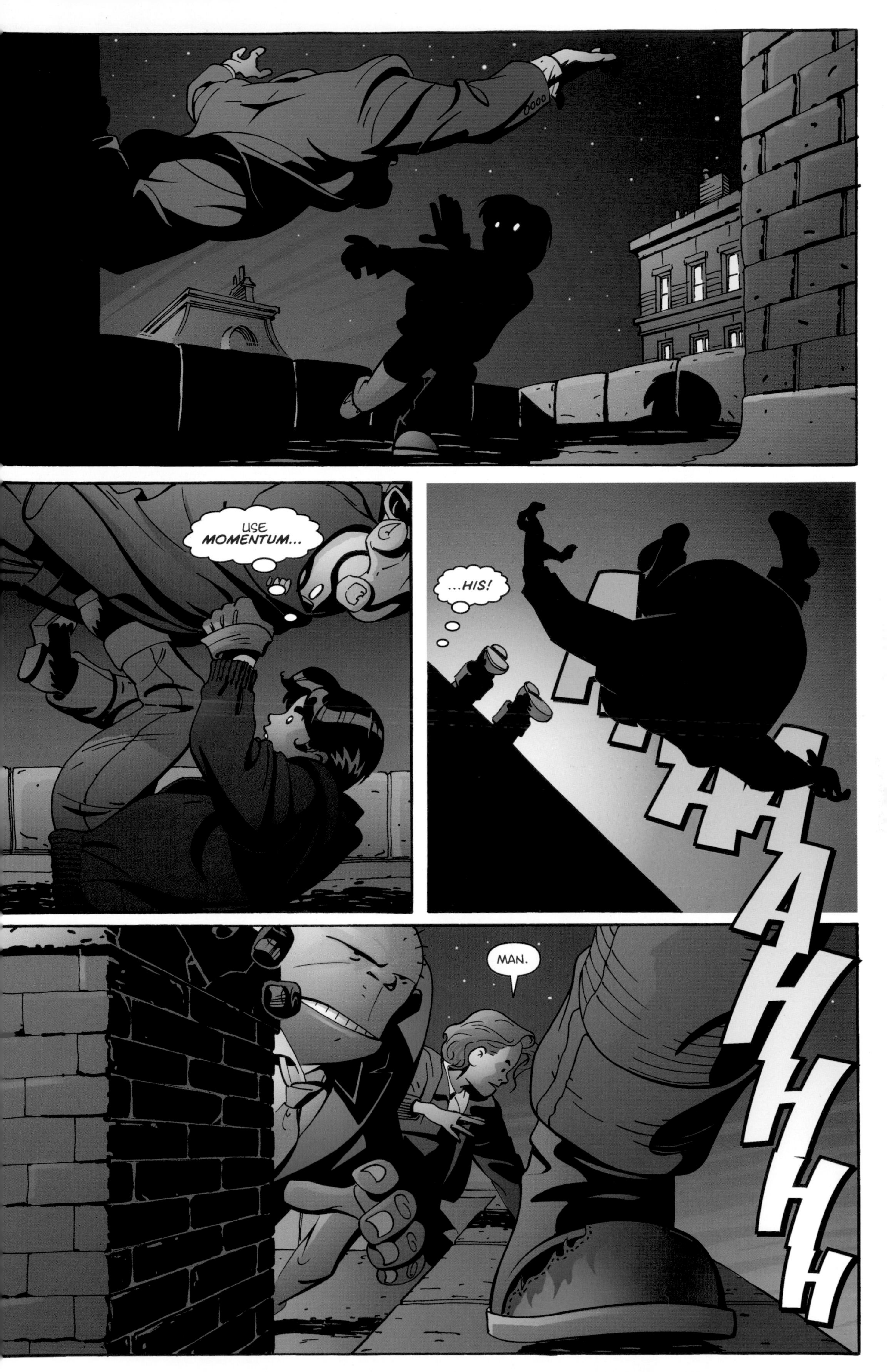
USE MOMENTUM...
...HIS!
MAN.

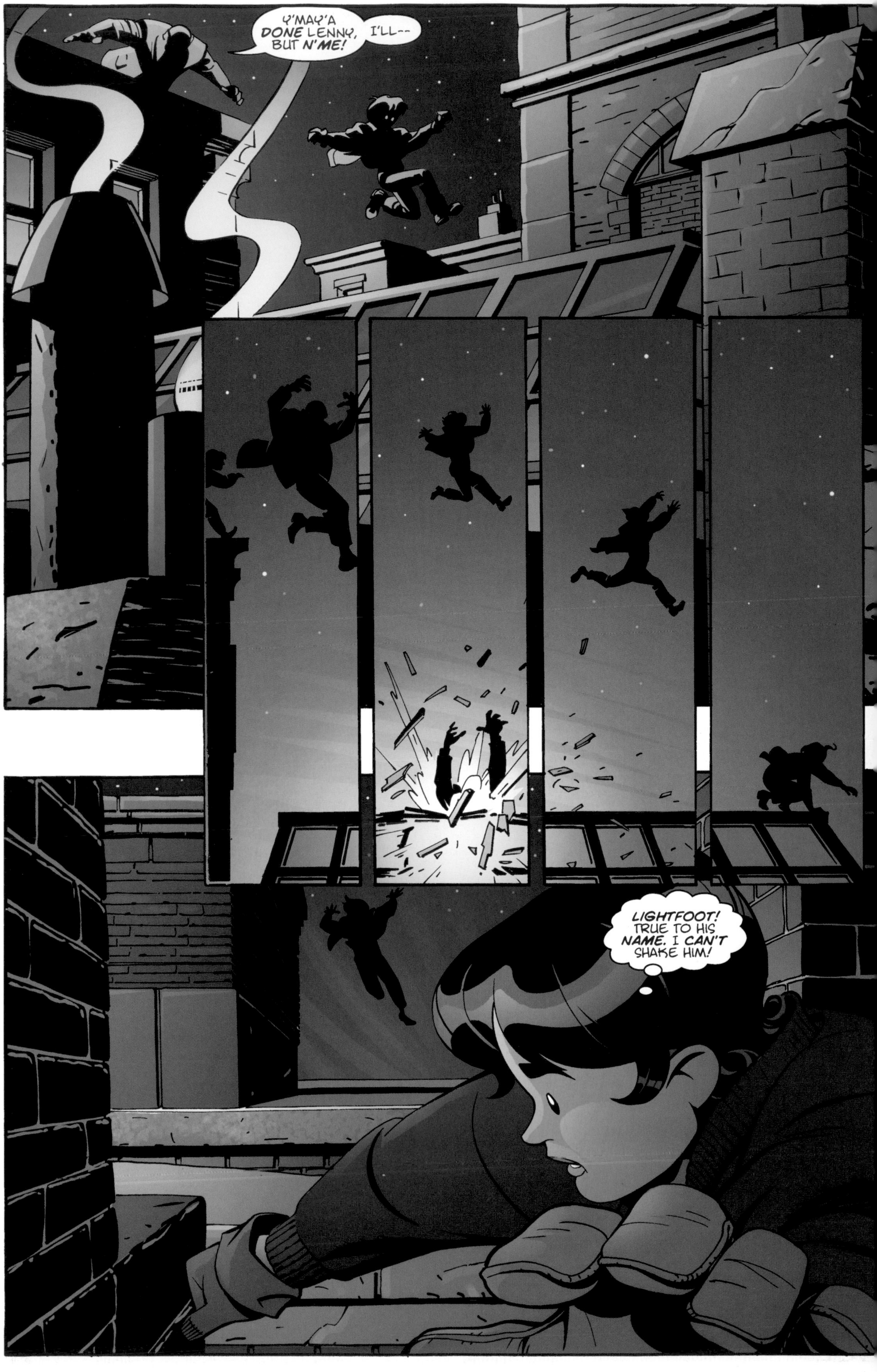
Y'MAY'A DONE LENNY, BUT N'ME! I'LL--
LIGHTFOOT! TRUE TO HIS NAME. I CAN'T SHAKE HIM!

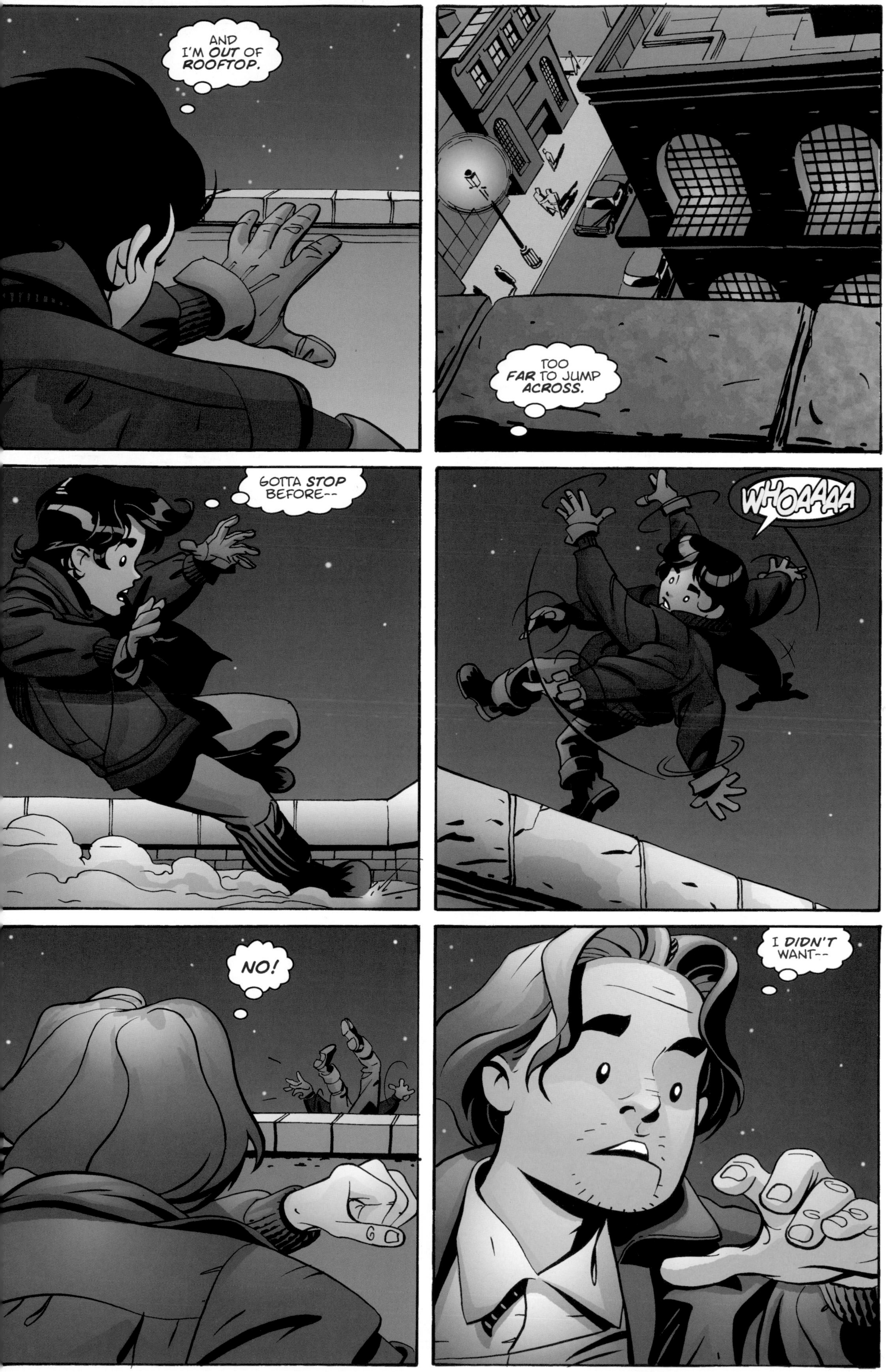
AND I'M OUT OF ROOFTOP.
TOO FAR TO JUMP ACROSS.
GOTTA STOP BEFORE--
WHOAAAA
NO!
I DIDN'T WANT--

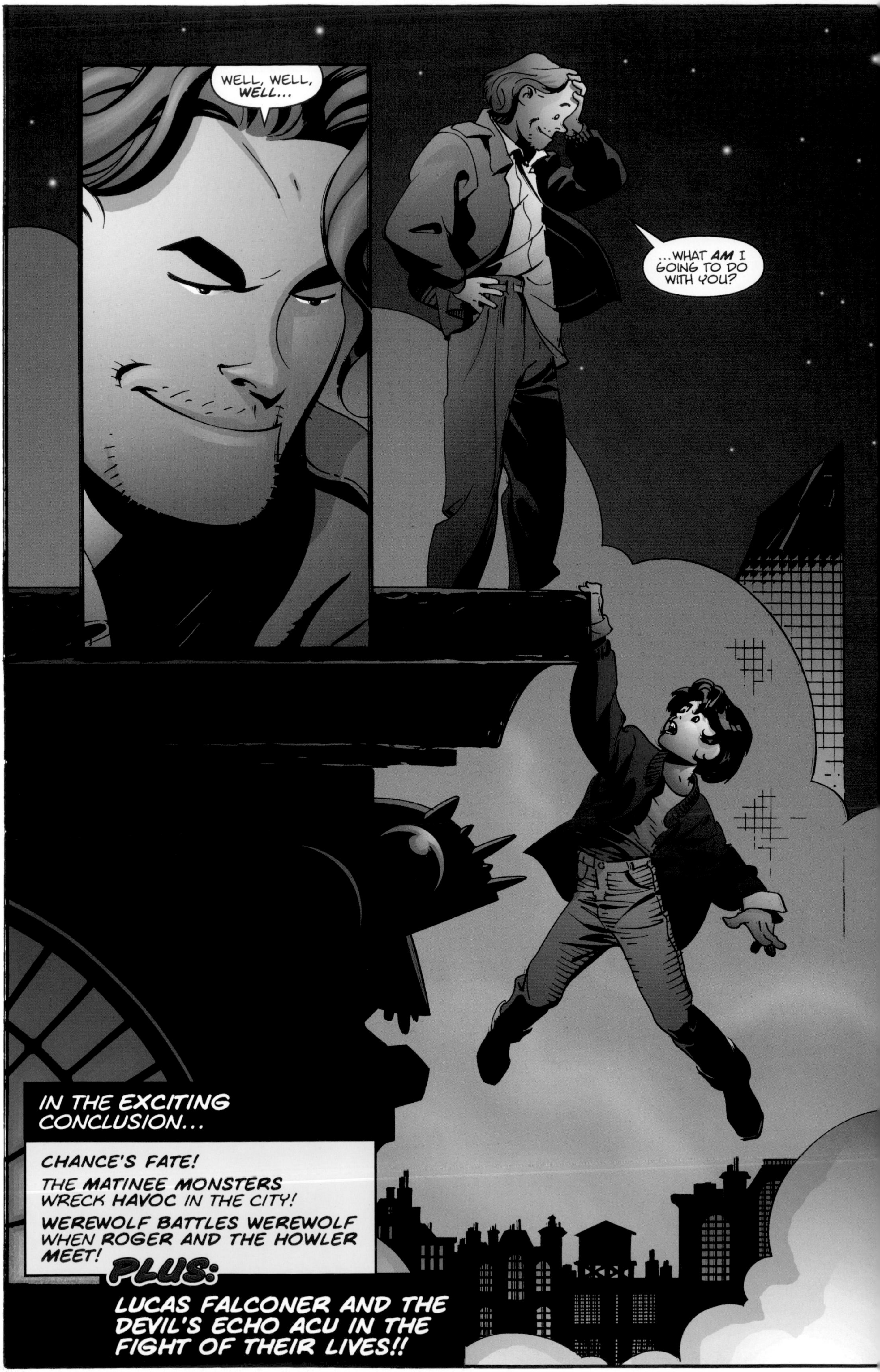
WELL, WELL, WELL...
...WHAT AM I GOING TO DO WITH YOU?
IN THE EXCITING CONCLUSION...
CHANCE'S FATE!
THE MATINEE MONSTERS WRECK HAVOC IN THE CITY!
WEREWOLF BATTLES WEREWOLF WHEN ROGER AND THE HOWLER MEET!
PLUS:
LUCAS FALCONER AND THE DEVIL'S ECHO ACU IN THE FIGHT OF THEIR LIVES!!

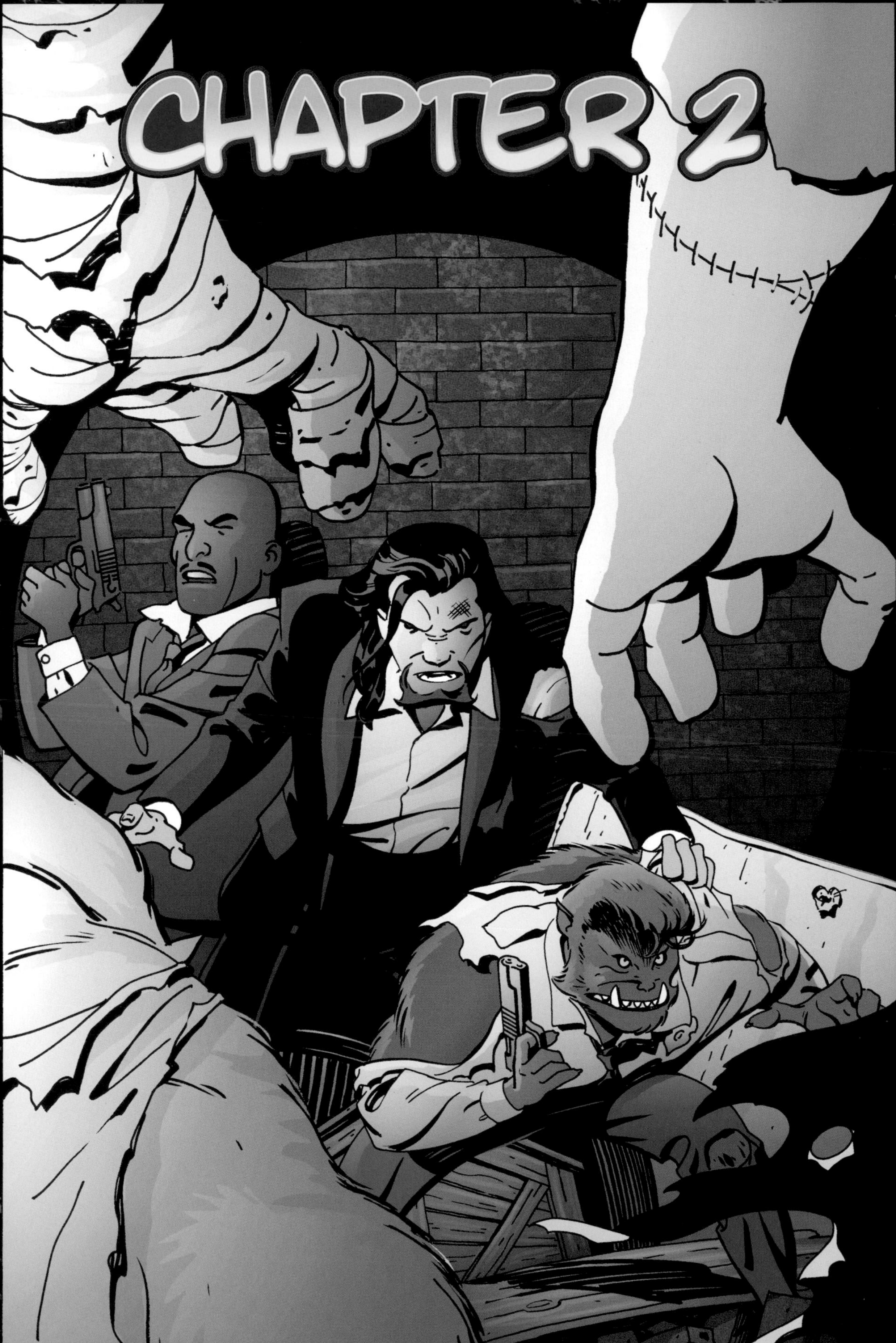
CHAPTER 2

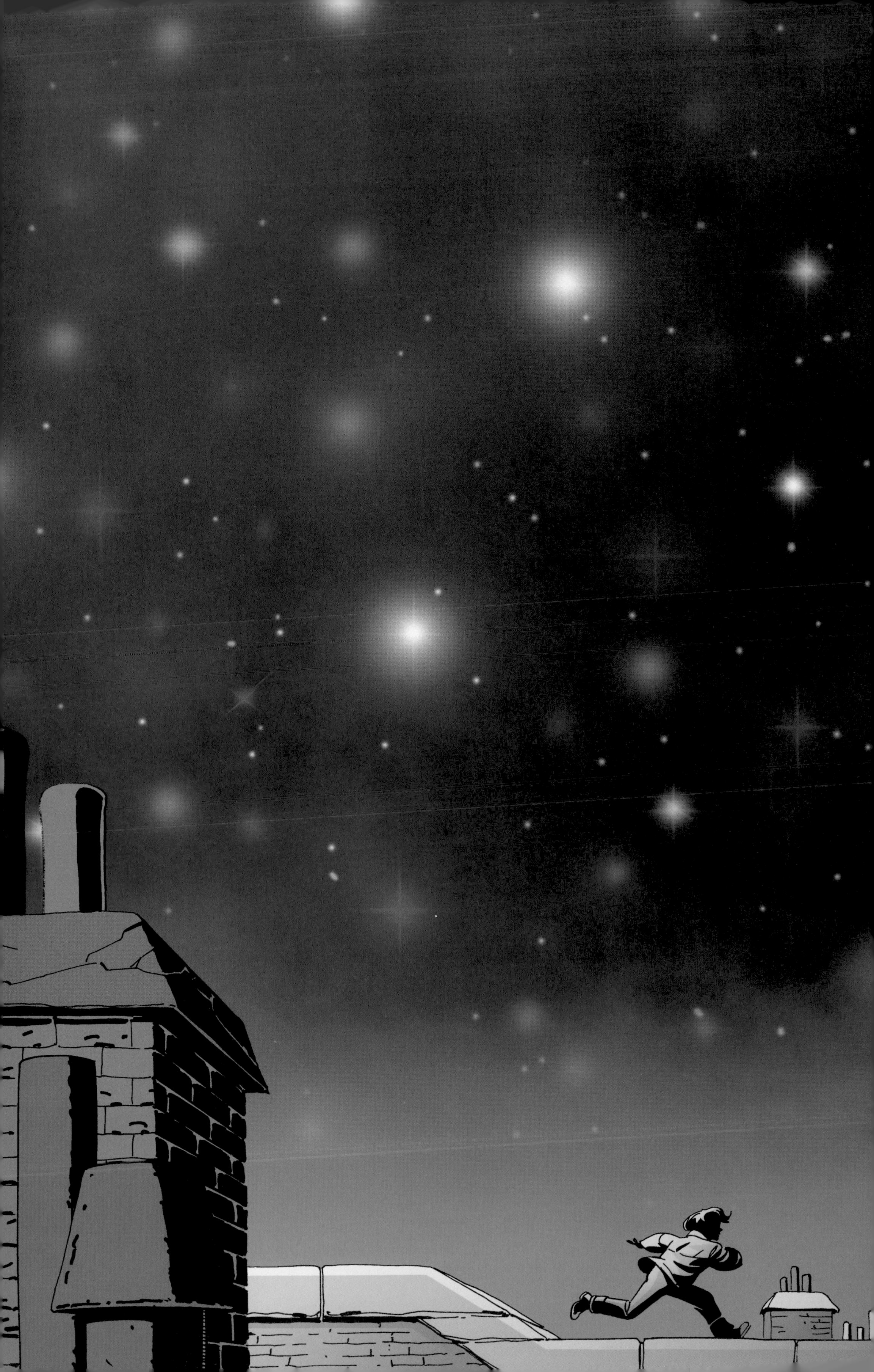

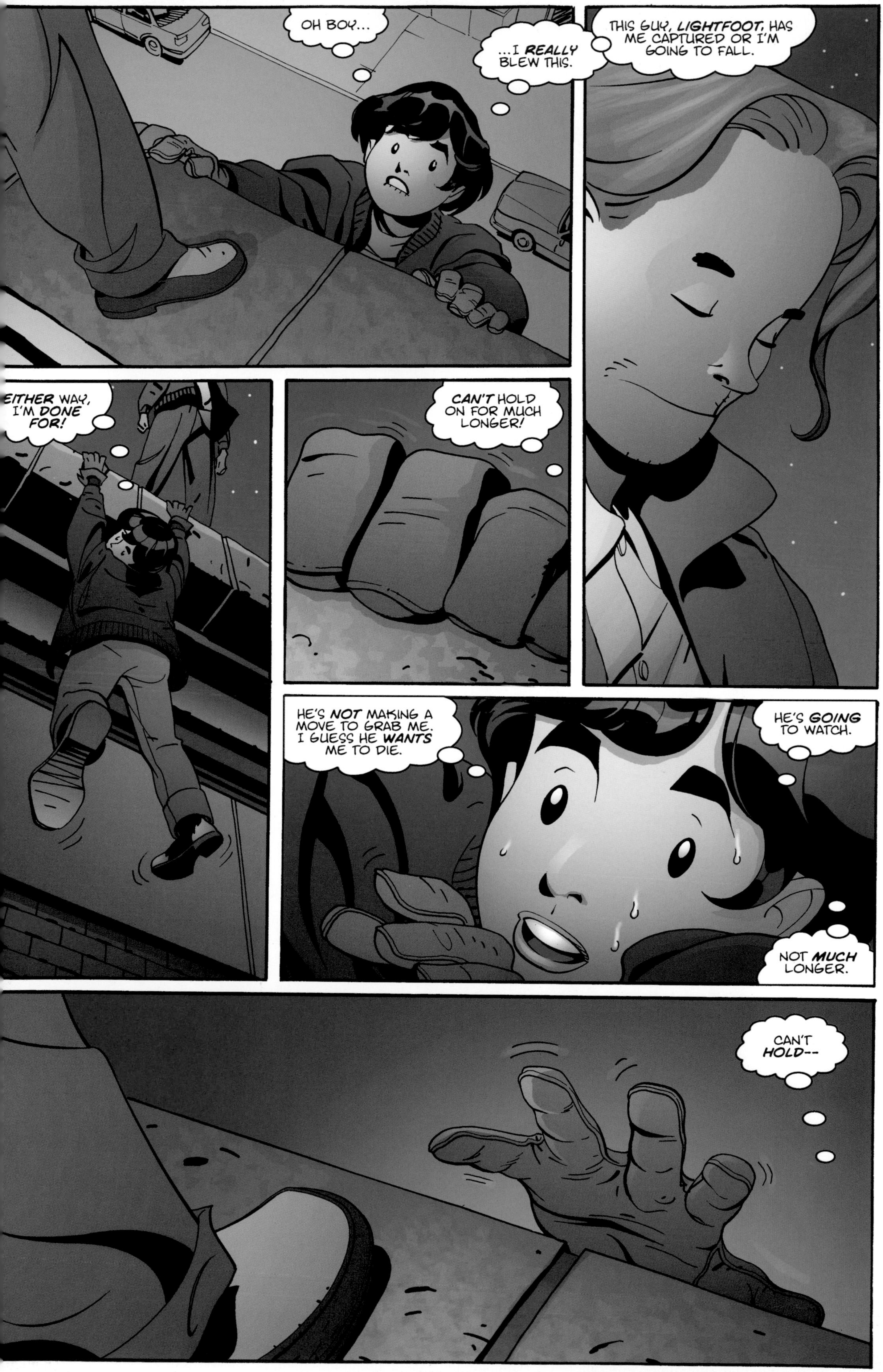
OH BOY...
...I REALLY BLEW THIS.
THIS GUY, LIGHTFOOT, HAS ME CAPTURED OR I'M GOING TO FALL.
EITHER WAY, I'M DONE FOR!
CAN'T HOLD ON FOR MUCH LONGER!
HE'S NOT MAKING A MOVE TO GRAB ME. I GUESS HE WANTS ME TO DIE.
HE'S GOING TO WATCH.
NOT MUCH LONGER.
CAN'T HOLD--

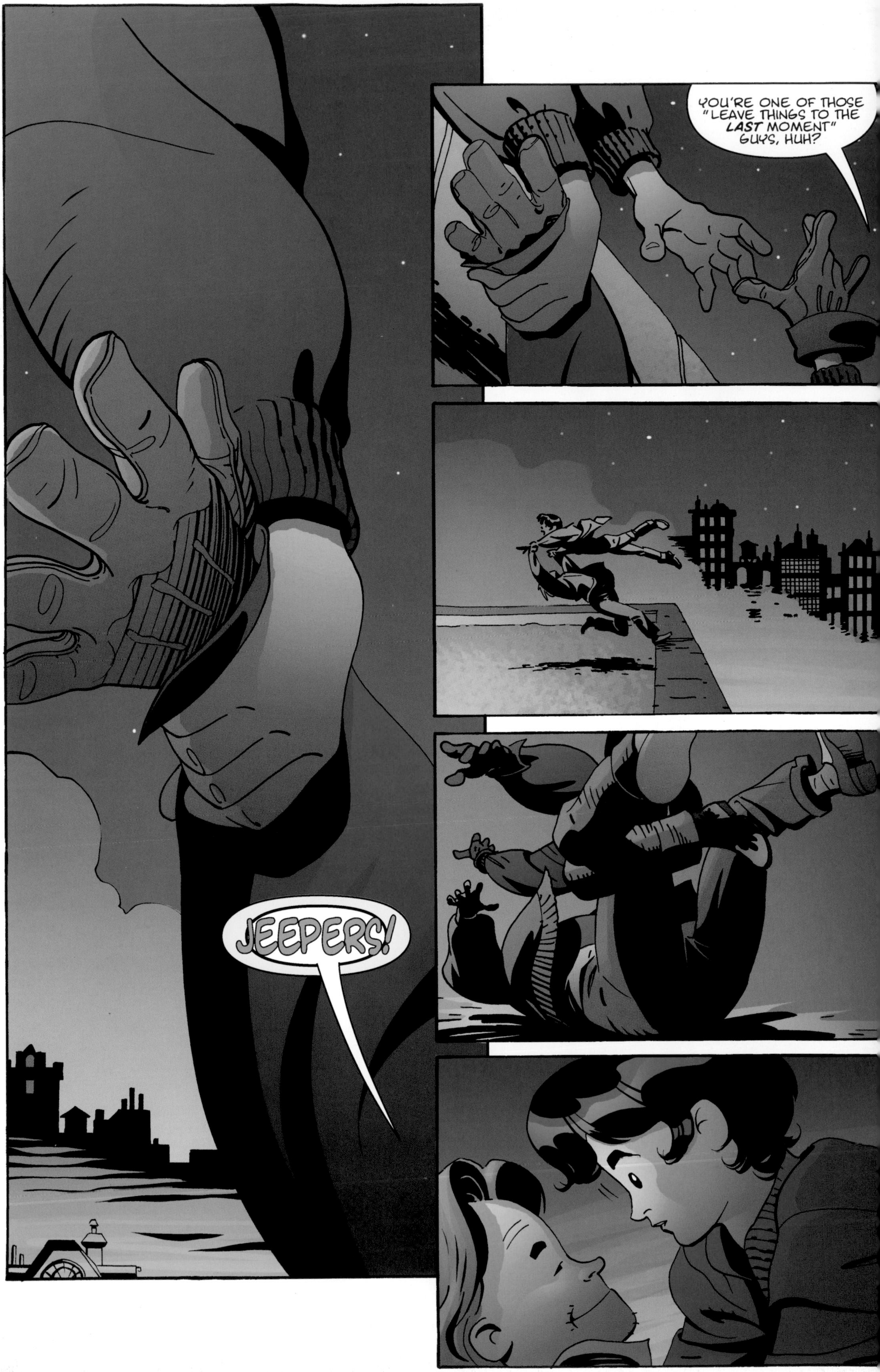
JEEPERS!
YOU'RE ONE OF THOSE "LEAVE THINGS TO THE LAST MOMENT" GUYS, HUH?

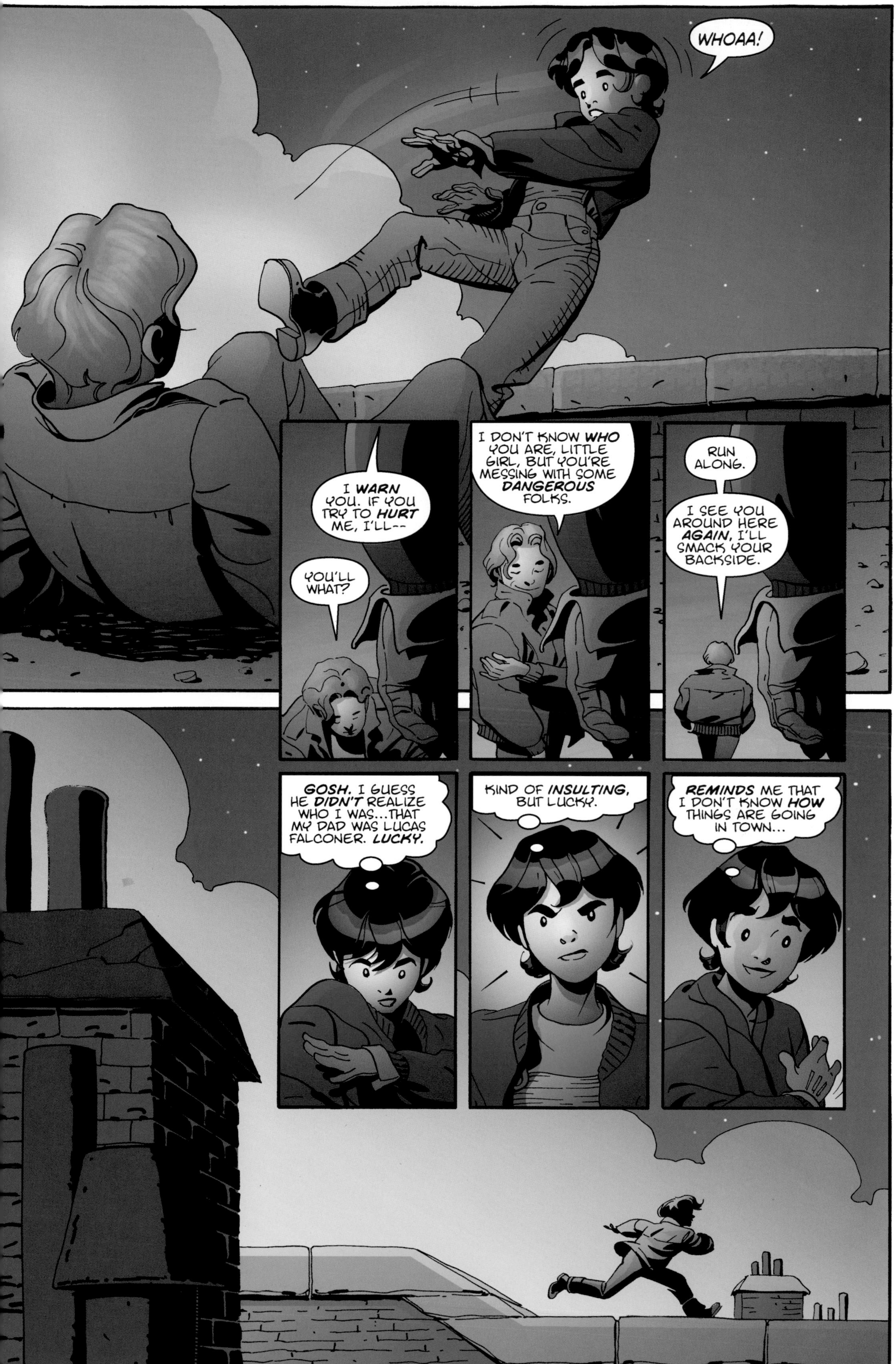
WHOAA!
I WARN YOU. IF YOU TRY TO HURT ME, I'LL--
YOU'LL WHAT?
I DON'T KNOW WHO YOU ARE, LITTLE GIRL, BUT YOU'RE MESSING WITH SOME DANGEROUS FOLKS.
RUN ALONG.
I SEE YOU AROUND HERE AGAIN, I'LL SMACK YOUR BACKSIDE.
GOSH. I GUESS HE DIDN'T REALIZE WHO I WAS...THAT MY DAD WAS LUCAS FALCONER. LUCKY.
KIND OF INSULTING, BUT LUCKY.
REMINDS ME THAT I DON'T KNOW HOW THINGS ARE GOING IN TOWN...

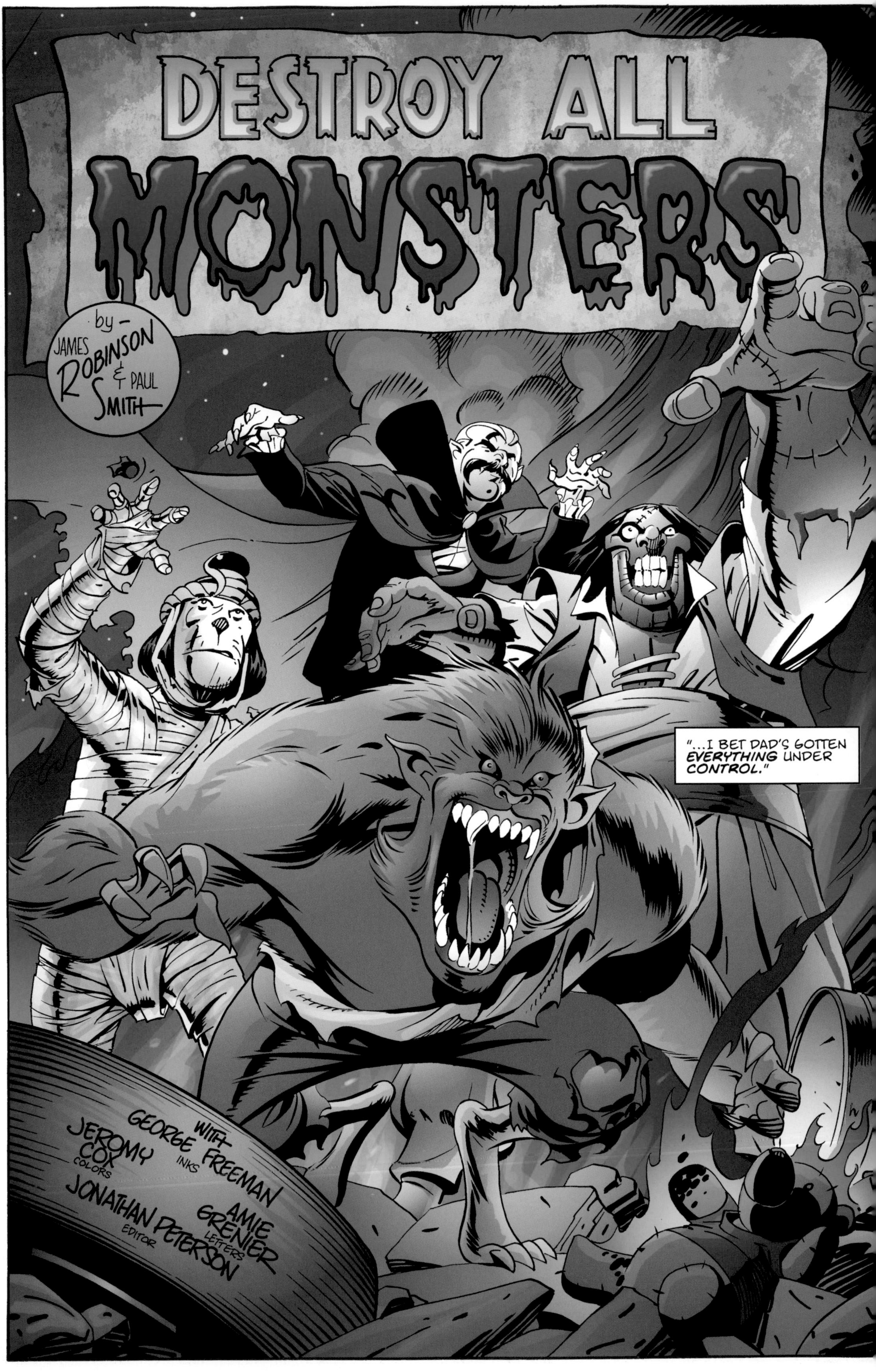
DESTROY ALL MONSTERS
by JAMES ROBINSON & PAUL SMITH
"...I BET DAD'S GOTTEN EVERYTHING UNDER CONTROL."
with GEORGE FREEMAN inks
JEROMY COX colors
AMIE GRENIER letters
JONATHAN PETERSON editor

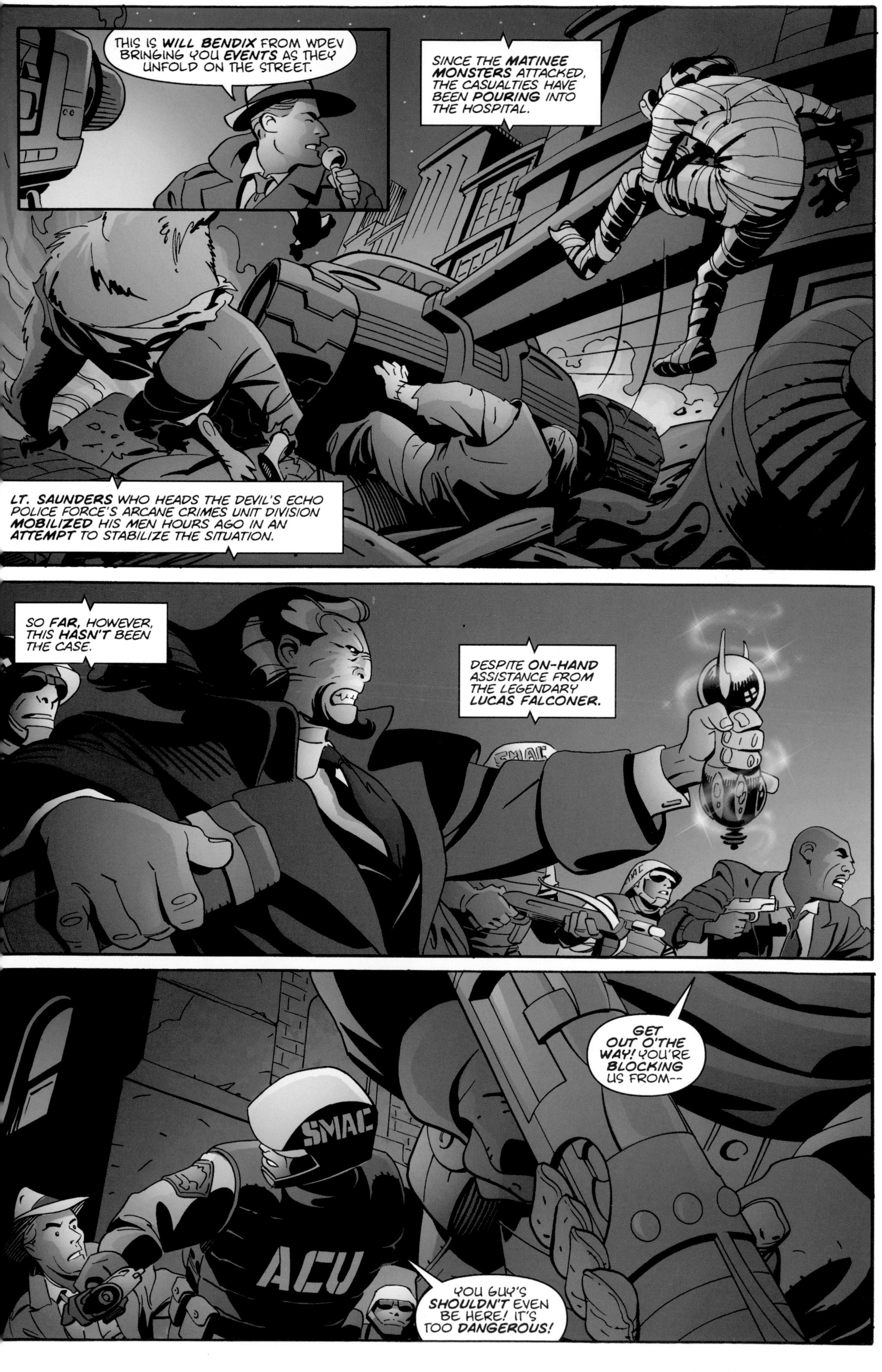

THIS IS WILL BENDIX FROM WDEV BRINGING YOU EVENTS AS THEY UNFOLD ON THE STREET.
SINCE THE MATINEE MONSTERS ATTACKED, THE CASUALTIES HAVE BEEN POURING INTO THE HOSPITAL.
LT. SAUNDERS WHO HEADS THE DEVIL'S ECHO POLICE FORCE'S ARCANE CRIMES UNIT DIVISION MOBILIZED HIS MEN HOURS AGO IN AN ATTEMPT TO STABILIZE THE SITUATION.
SO FAR, HOWEVER, THIS HASN'T BEEN THE CASE.
DESPITE ON-HAND ASSISTANCE FROM THE LEGENDARY LUCAS FALCONER.
GET OUT O'THE WAY! YOU'RE BLOCKING US FROM--
SMAC
ACU
YOU GUY'S SHOULDN'T EVEN BE HERE! IT'S TOO DANGEROUS!

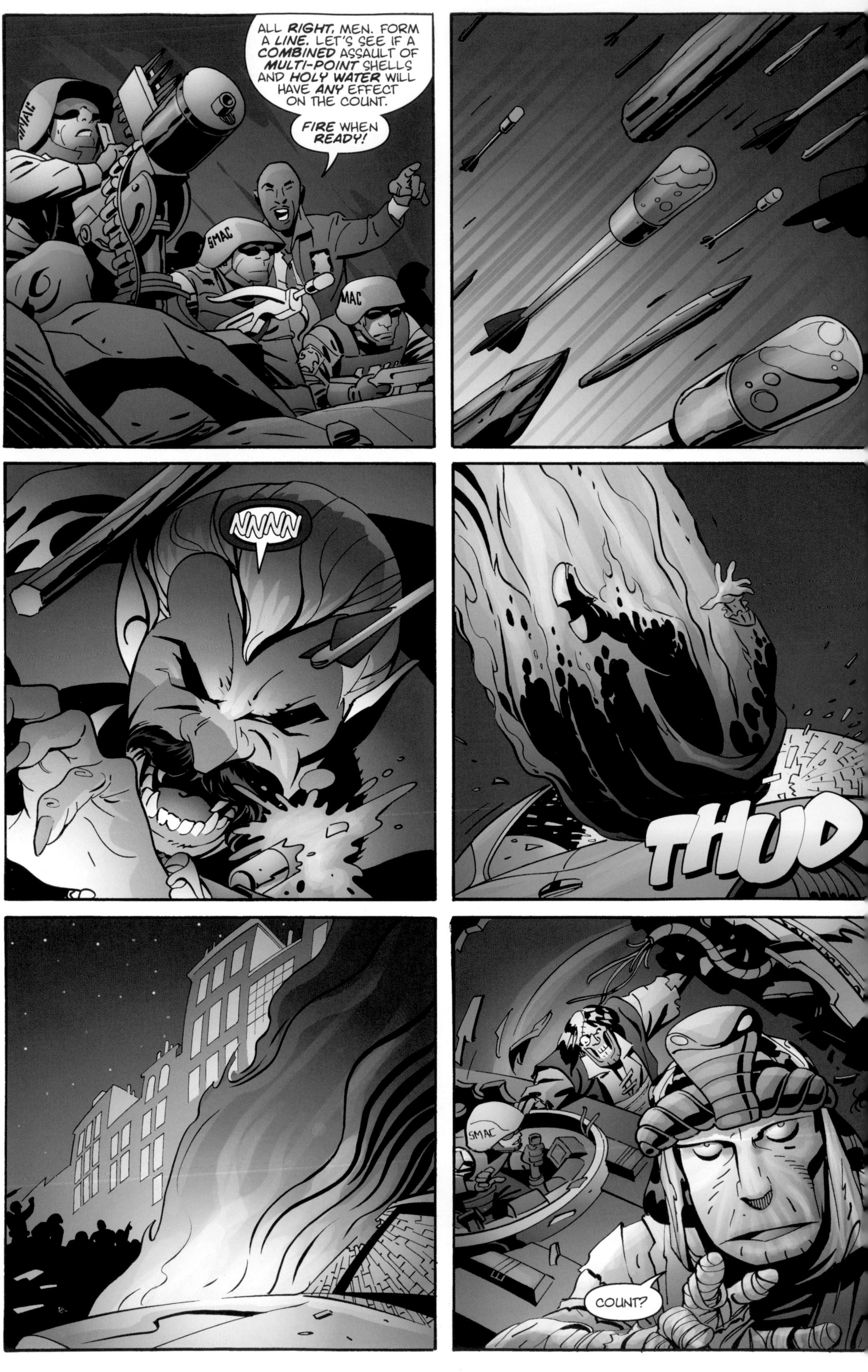
ALL RIGHT, MEN. FORM A LINE. LET'S SEE IF A COMBINED ASSAULT OF MULTI-POINT SHELLS AND HOLY WATER WILL HAVE ANY EFFECT ON THE COUNT.
FIRE WHEN READY!
SMAC
SMAC
MAC
NNNN
THUD
SMAC
COUNT?

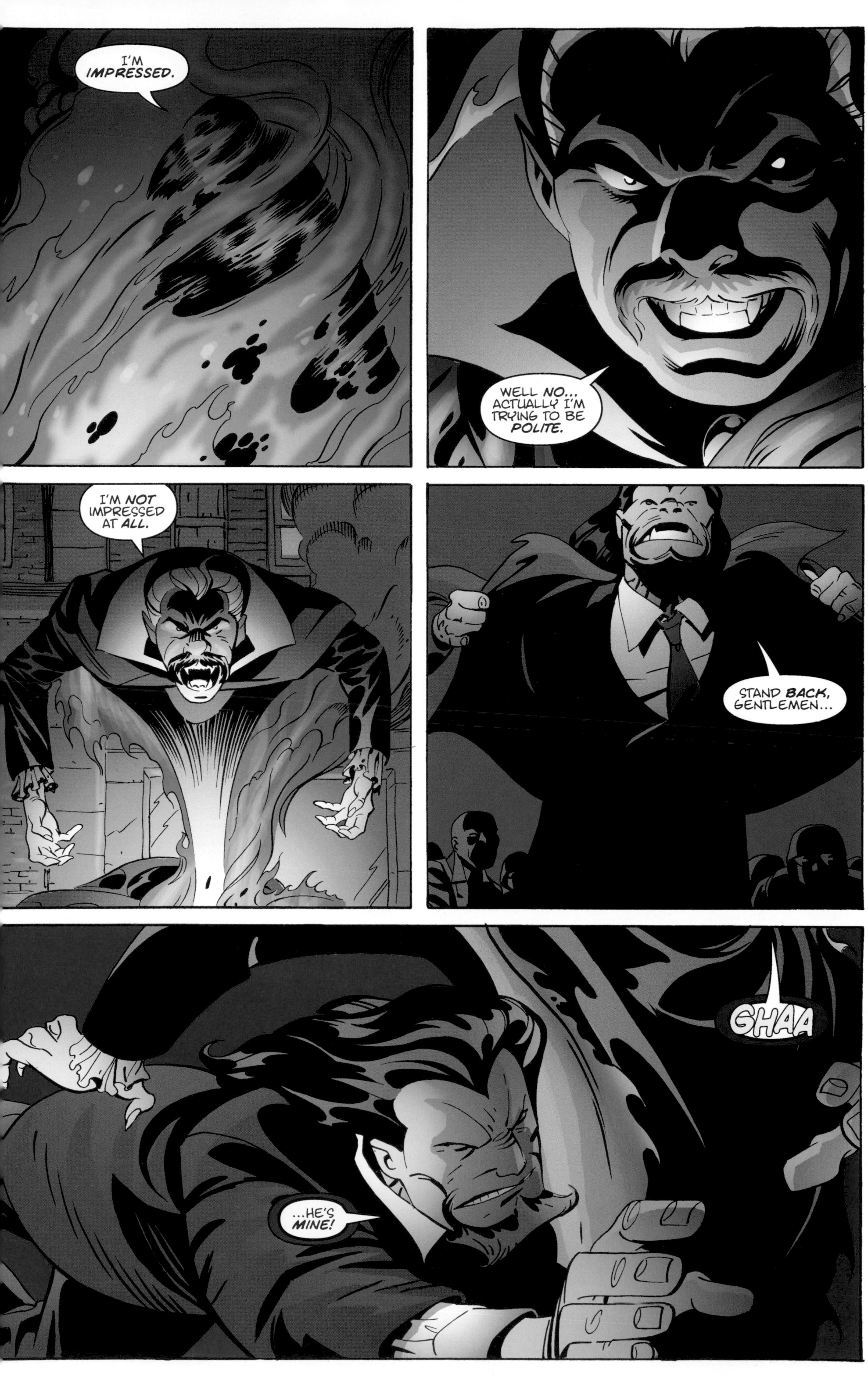

I'M IMPRESSED.
WELL NO... ACTUALLY I'M TRYING TO BE POLITE.
I'M NOT IMPRESSED AT ALL.
STAND BACK, GENTLEMEN...
SHAA
...HE'S MINE!

AHH, *LUCAS FALCONER* ARMED WITH WHAT I PRESUME IS A--

MULTI-FAITH *TALISMAN!* KEEP BACK *MONSTER!*

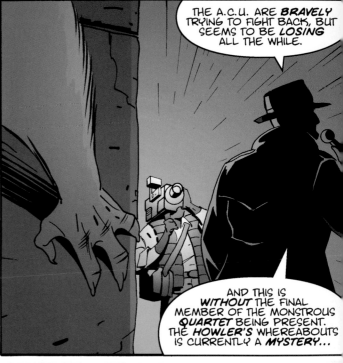

IT *WAS* A TALISMAN.

NOW IT'S *ABSTRACT ART.*

CRUNCH!

--TINUE WITH WILL BENDIX'S *LIVE* REPORT.

AS LUCAS *STANDS* HIS GROUND AGAINST THE COUNT, SO *MAN-MONSTER* AND *PHARAOH* WAGE A *RUTHLESS* RAMPAGE NEARBY.

13 WDEV

THE A.C.U. ARE *BRAVELY* TRYING TO FIGHT BACK, BUT SEEMS TO BE *LOSING* ALL THE WHILE.

AND THIS IS *WITHOUT* THE FINAL MEMBER OF THE MONSTROUS *QUARTET* BEING PRESENT. THE *HOWLER'S* WHEREABOUTS IS CURRENTLY A *MYSTERY...*

...ALTHOUGH WE CAN BE *CERTAIN* THE WEREWOLF WILL *REAPPEAR* AT ANY MOME--*ARHHHH*

GRRRRR

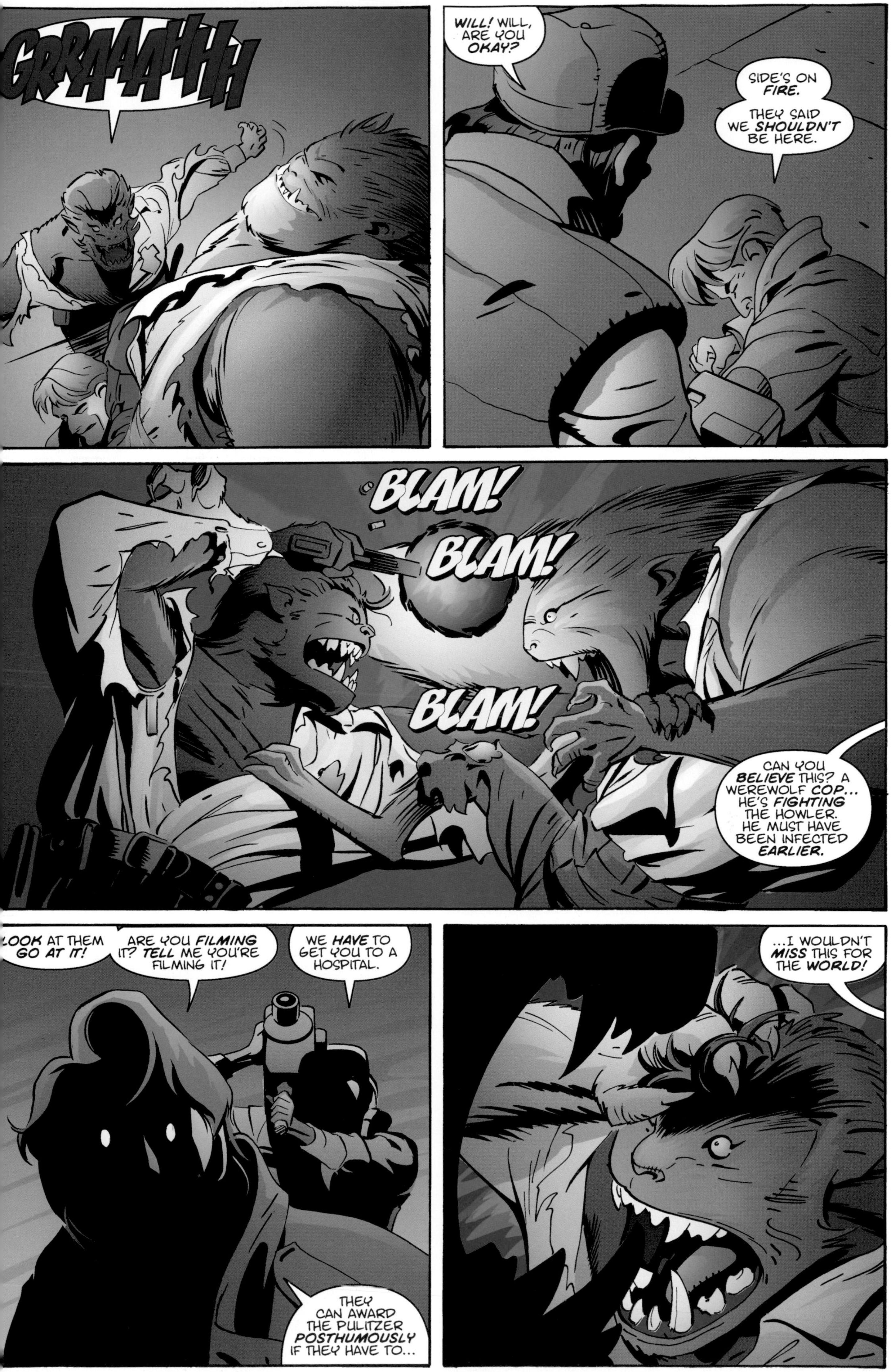
GRRAAAHHH
WILL! WILL, ARE YOU OKAY?
SIDE'S ON FIRE.
THEY SAID WE SHOULDN'T BE HERE.
BLAM!
BLAM!
BLAM!
CAN YOU BELIEVE THIS? A WEREWOLF COP... HE'S FIGHTING THE HOWLER. HE MUST HAVE BEEN INFECTED EARLIER.
LOOK AT THEM GO AT IT!
ARE YOU FILMING IT? TELL ME YOU'RE FILMING IT!
WE HAVE TO GET YOU TO A HOSPITAL.
THEY CAN AWARD THE PULITZER POSTHUMOUSLY IF THEY HAVE TO...
...I WOULDN'T MISS THIS FOR THE WORLD!

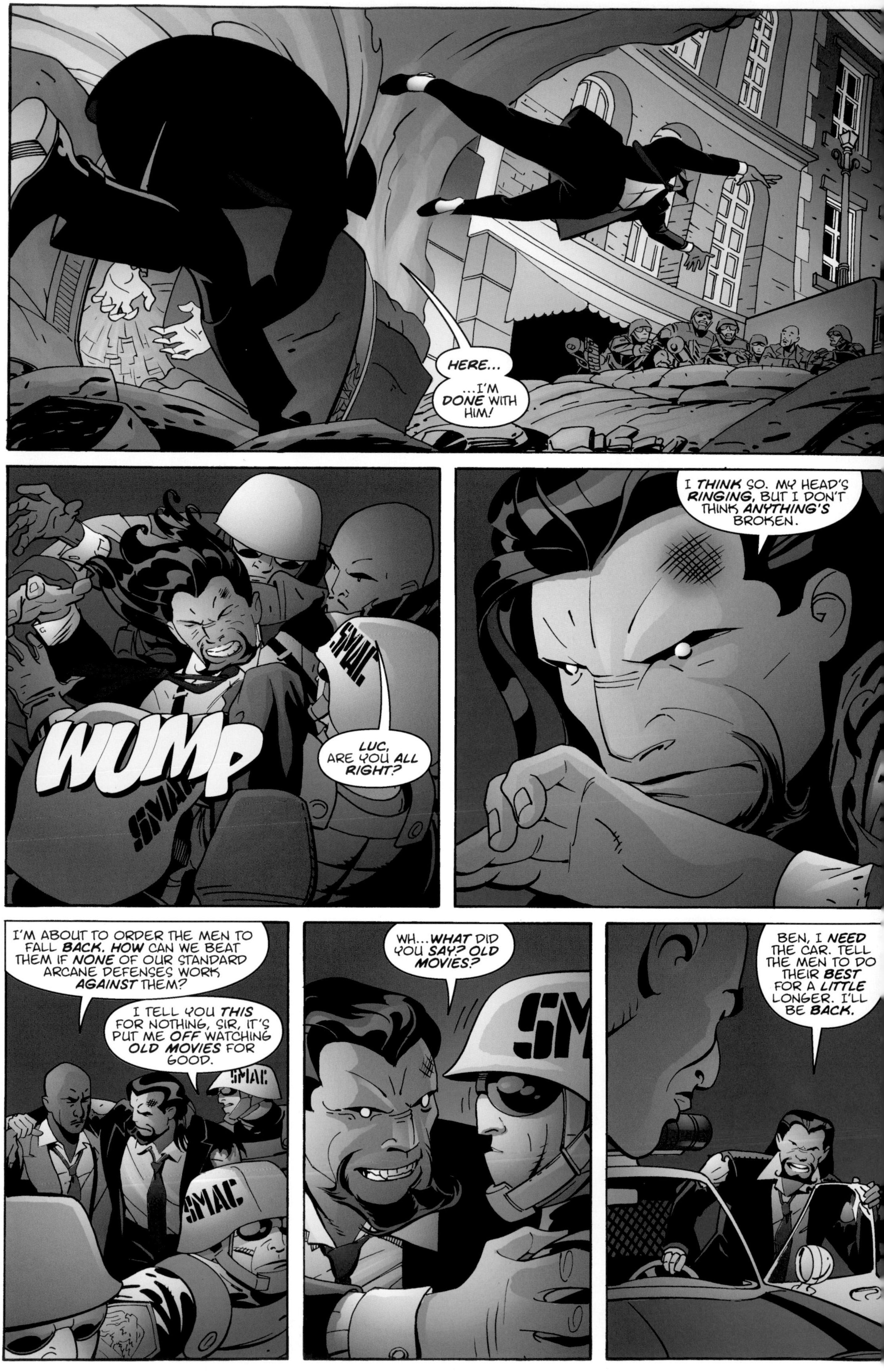
HERE...
...I'M DONE WITH HIM!
WUMP
LUC, ARE YOU ALL RIGHT?
SMAC
I THINK SO. MY HEAD'S RINGING, BUT I DON'T THINK ANYTHING'S BROKEN.
I'M ABOUT TO ORDER THE MEN TO FALL BACK. HOW CAN WE BEAT THEM IF NONE OF OUR STANDARD ARCANE DEFENSES WORK AGAINST THEM?
I TELL YOU THIS FOR NOTHING, SIR, IT'S PUT ME OFF WATCHING OLD MOVIES FOR GOOD.
WH...WHAT DID YOU SAY? OLD MOVIES?
BEN, I NEED THE CAR. TELL THE MEN TO DO THEIR BEST FOR A LITTLE LONGER. I'LL BE BACK.

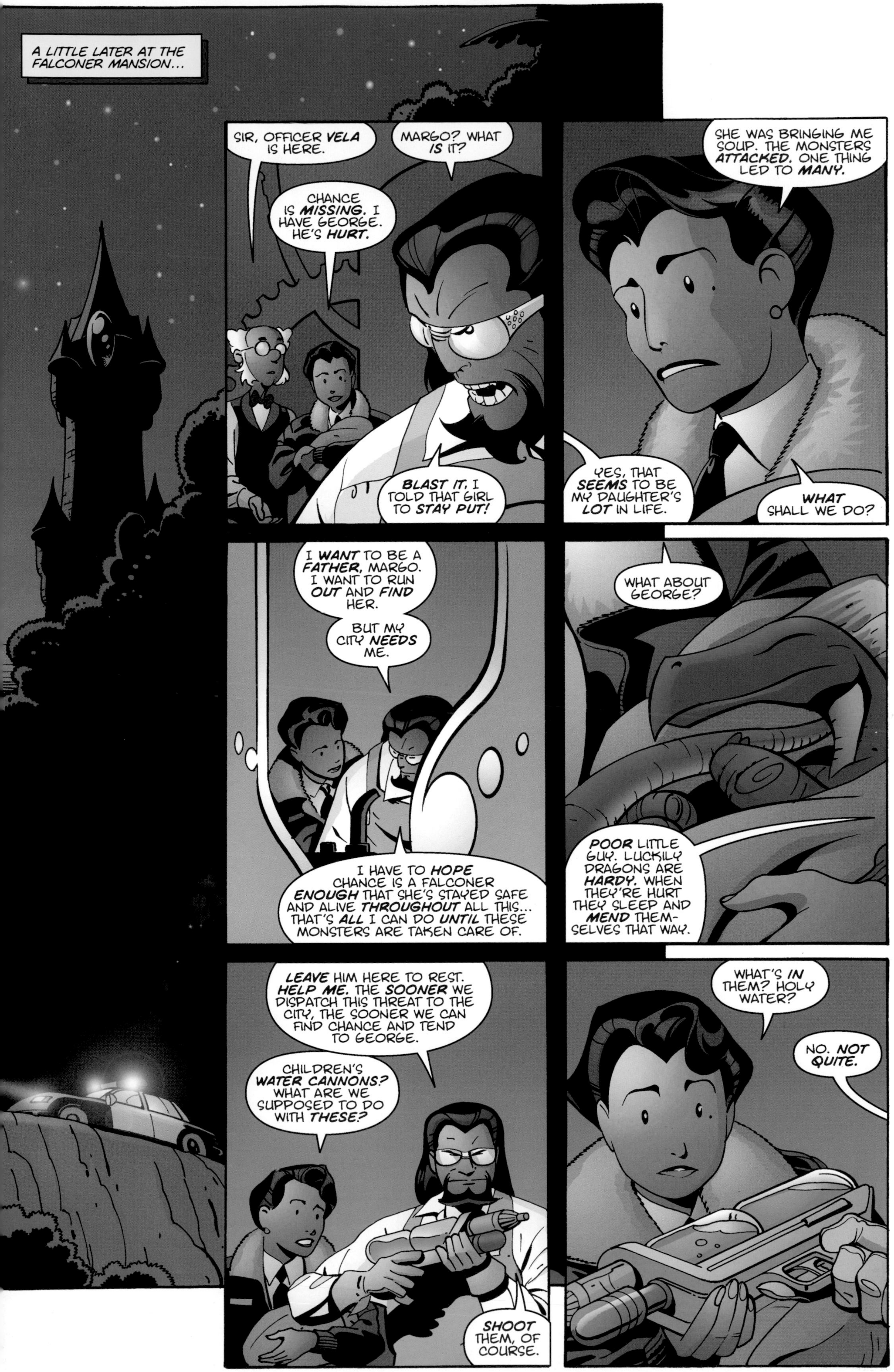
A LITTLE LATER AT THE FALCONER MANSION...
SIR, OFFICER VELA IS HERE.
MARGO? WHAT IS IT?
CHANCE IS MISSING. I HAVE GEORGE. HE'S HURT.
BLAST IT, I TOLD THAT GIRL TO STAY PUT!
SHE WAS BRINGING ME SOUP. THE MONSTERS ATTACKED. ONE THING LED TO MANY.
YES, THAT SEEMS TO BE MY DAUGHTER'S LOT IN LIFE.
WHAT SHALL WE DO?
I WANT TO BE A FATHER, MARGO. I WANT TO RUN OUT AND FIND HER.
BUT MY CITY NEEDS ME.
I HAVE TO HOPE CHANCE IS A FALCONER ENOUGH THAT SHE'S STAYED SAFE AND ALIVE THROUGHOUT ALL THIS... THAT'S ALL I CAN DO UNTIL THESE MONSTERS ARE TAKEN CARE OF.
WHAT ABOUT GEORGE?
POOR LITTLE GUY. LUCKILY DRAGONS ARE HARDY. WHEN THEY'RE HURT THEY SLEEP AND MEND THEMSELVES THAT WAY.
LEAVE HIM HERE TO REST. HELP ME. THE SOONER WE DISPATCH THIS THREAT TO THE CITY, THE SOONER WE CAN FIND CHANCE AND TEND TO GEORGE.
CHILDREN'S WATER CANNONS? WHAT ARE WE SUPPOSED TO DO WITH THESE?
SHOOT THEM, OF COURSE.
WHAT'S IN THEM? HOLY WATER?
NO. NOT QUITE.

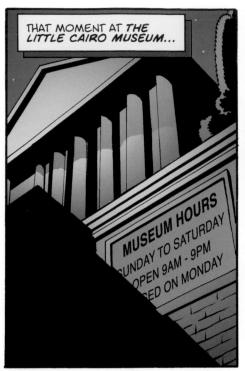

THAT MOMENT AT *THE LITTLE CAIRO MUSEUM...*

MUSEUM HOURS
SUNDAY TO SATURDAY
OPEN 9AM - 9PM
CLOSED ON MONDAY

BEEP BEEP BEEP BEEP BEEP BEEP

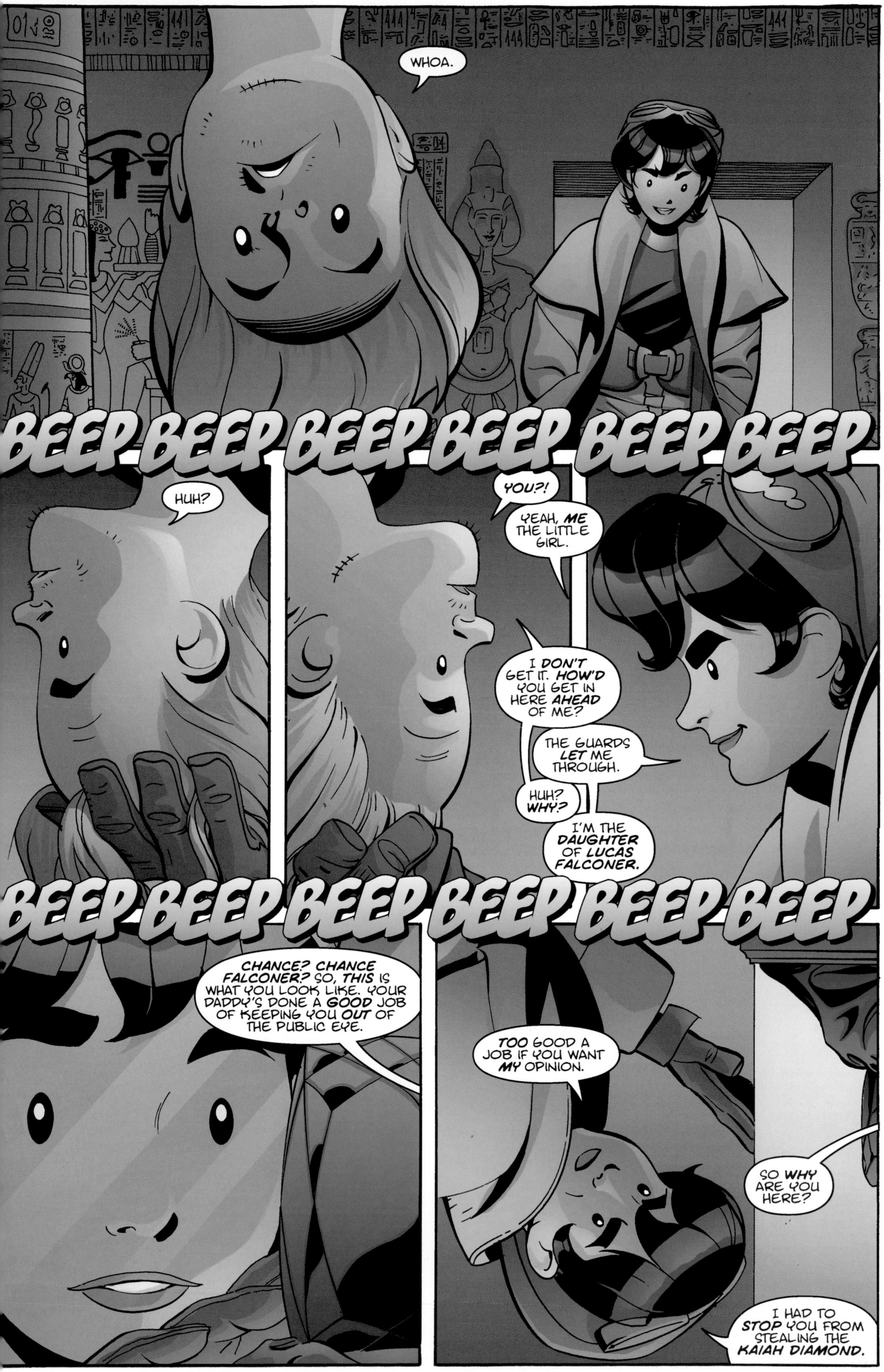
WHOA.
BEEP BEEP BEEP BEEP BEEP BEEP
HUH?
YOU?!
YEAH, ME THE LITTLE GIRL.
I DON'T GET IT. HOW'D YOU GET IN HERE AHEAD OF ME?
THE GUARDS LET ME THROUGH.
HUH? WHY?
I'M THE DAUGHTER OF LUCAS FALCONER.
BEEP BEEP BEEP BEEP BEEP BEEP
CHANCE? CHANCE FALCONER? SO, THIS IS WHAT YOU LOOK LIKE. YOUR DADDY'S DONE A GOOD JOB OF KEEPING YOU OUT OF THE PUBLIC EYE.
TOO GOOD A JOB IF YOU WANT MY OPINION.
SO WHY ARE YOU HERE?
I HAD TO STOP YOU FROM STEALING THE KAIAH DIAMOND.

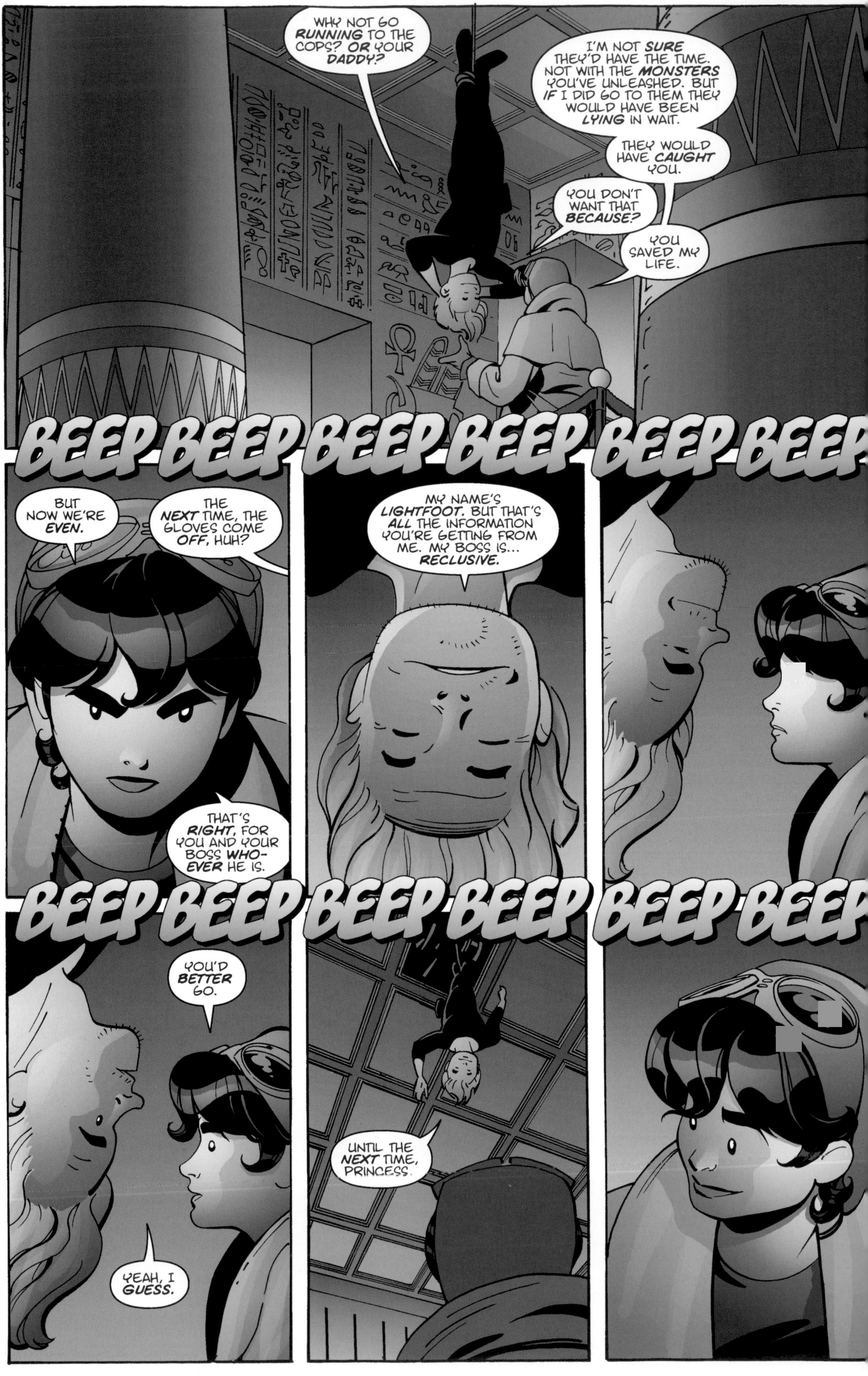
WHY NOT GO RUNNING TO THE COPS? OR YOUR DADDY?
I'M NOT SURE THEY'D HAVE THE TIME. NOT WITH THE MONSTERS YOU'VE UNLEASHED. BUT IF I DID GO TO THEM THEY WOULD HAVE BEEN LYING IN WAIT.
THEY WOULD HAVE CAUGHT YOU.
YOU DON'T WANT THAT BECAUSE?
YOU SAVED MY LIFE.
BEEP BEEP BEEP BEEP BEEP BEEP
BUT NOW WE'RE EVEN.
THE NEXT TIME, THE GLOVES COME OFF, HUH?
THAT'S RIGHT, FOR YOU AND YOUR BOSS WHO-EVER HE IS.
MY NAME'S LIGHTFOOT. BUT THAT'S ALL THE INFORMATION YOU'RE GETTING FROM ME. MY BOSS IS... RECLUSIVE.
BEEP BEEP BEEP BEEP BEEP BEEP
YOU'D BETTER GO.
YEAH, I GUESS.
UNTIL THE NEXT TIME, PRINCESS.

THOK!

WHAT A *MAGNIFICENT* SPECIMEN.

WONDER IF WE COULD *REASON* WITH HIM. HE'D BE A *WONDERFUL* ADDITION TO--

NO. IT DOESN'T LOOK VERY *REASONABLE*. IT'S BEST WE SIMPLY *ATTACK* AND--

IT ENDS *NOW...*

...OR WE *DESTROY ALL MONSTERS!*

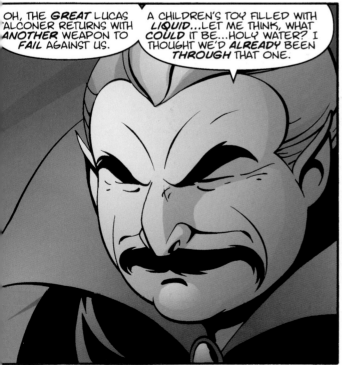

OH, THE *GREAT* LUCAS FALCONER RETURNS WITH *ANOTHER* WEAPON TO *FAIL* AGAINST US.

A CHILDREN'S TOY FILLED WITH *LIQUID*...LET ME THINK, WHAT *COULD* IT BE...HOLY WATER? I THOUGHT WE'D *ALREADY* BEEN *THROUGH* THAT ONE.

SOME *POTION*...A MIXTURE OF *BLESSED* HERBED AND *ARCANE* BALMS PERHAPS? YOU CAN *TRY*, BUT I WOULDN'T MAKE ANY *SUBSTANTIAL* BETS ON IT WORKING.

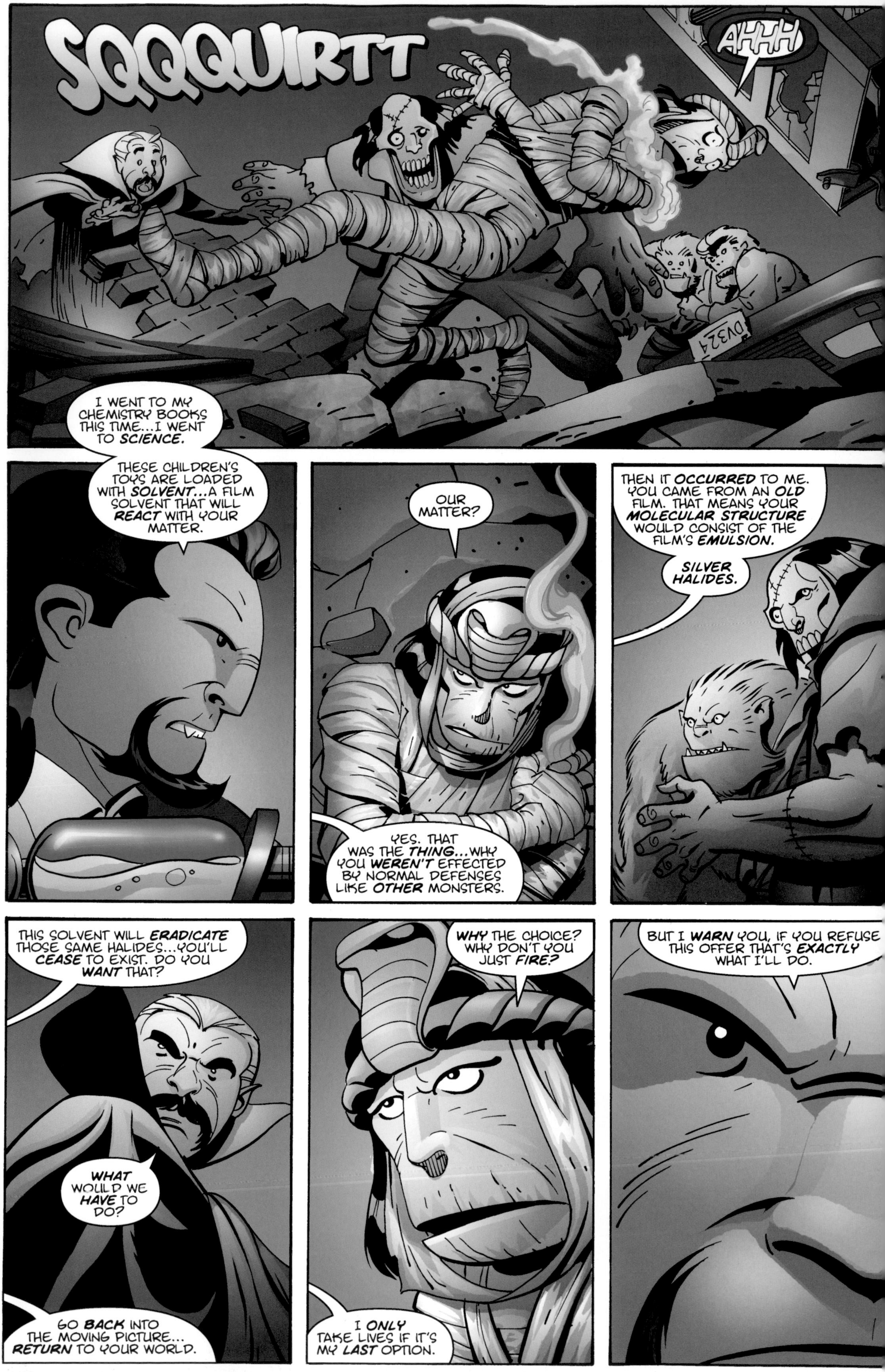
SQQQUIRTT
AHHH
I WENT TO MY CHEMISTRY BOOKS THIS TIME...I WENT TO SCIENCE.
THESE CHILDREN'S TOYS ARE LOADED WITH SOLVENT...A FILM SOLVENT THAT WILL REACT WITH YOUR MATTER.
OUR MATTER?
YES. THAT WAS THE THING...WHY YOU WEREN'T EFFECTED BY NORMAL DEFENSES LIKE OTHER MONSTERS.
THEN IT OCCURRED TO ME. YOU CAME FROM AN OLD FILM. THAT MEANS YOUR MOLECULAR STRUCTURE WOULD CONSIST OF THE FILM'S EMULSION.
SILVER HALIDES.
THIS SOLVENT WILL ERADICATE THOSE SAME HALIDES...YOU'LL CEASE TO EXIST. DO YOU WANT THAT?
WHAT WOULD WE HAVE TO DO?
GO BACK INTO THE MOVING PICTURE... RETURN TO YOUR WORLD.
WHY THE CHOICE? WHY DON'T YOU JUST FIRE?
I ONLY TAKE LIVES IF IT'S MY LAST OPTION.
BUT I WARN YOU, IF YOU REFUSE THIS OFFER THAT'S EXACTLY WHAT I'LL DO.

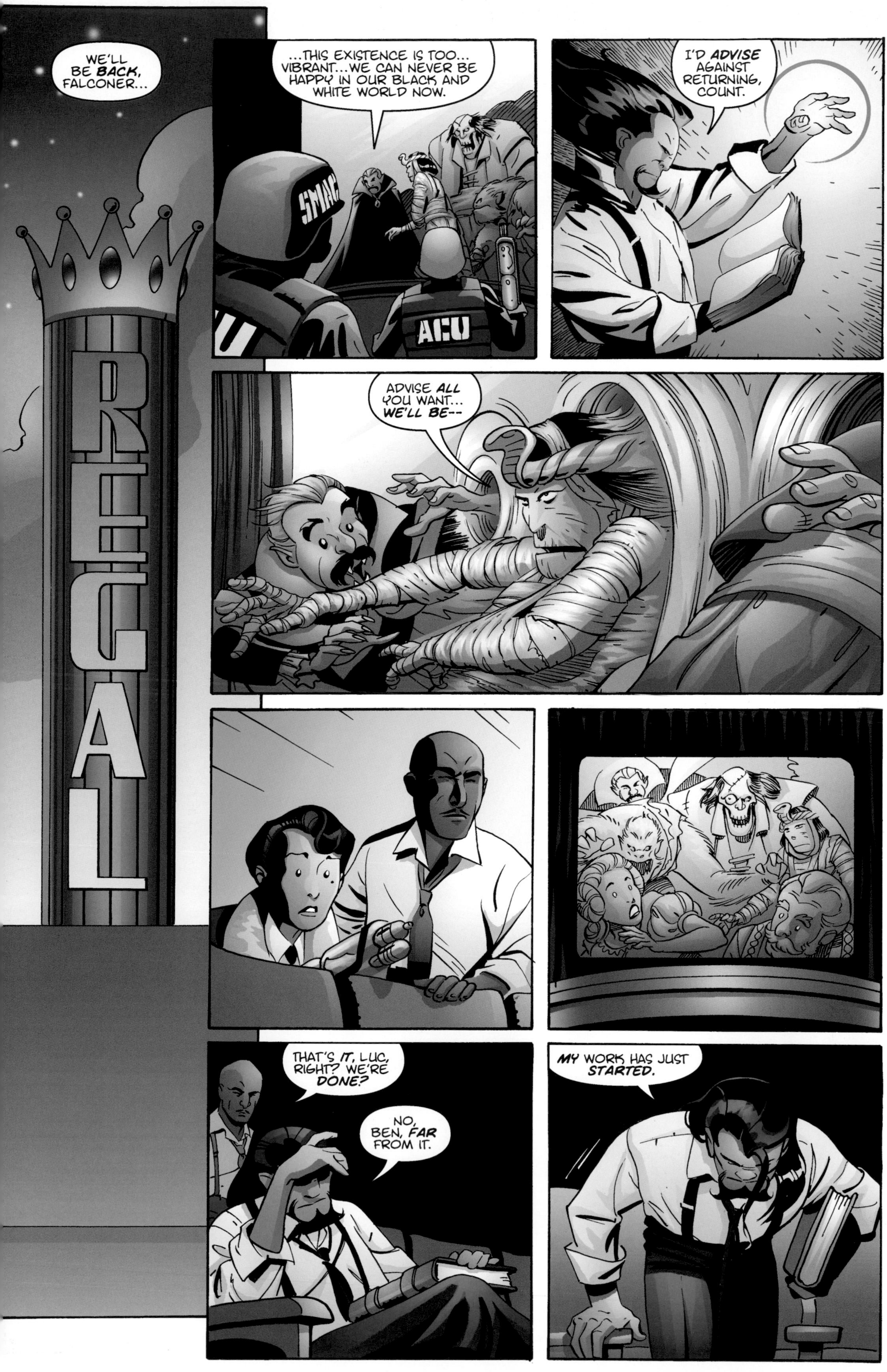
WE'LL BE BACK, FALCONER...
...THIS EXISTENCE IS TOO... VIBRANT...WE CAN NEVER BE HAPPY IN OUR BLACK AND WHITE WORLD NOW.
SMAC
ACU
I'D ADVISE AGAINST RETURNING, COUNT.
REGAL
ADVISE ALL YOU WANT... WE'LL BE--
THAT'S IT, LUC, RIGHT? WE'RE DONE?
NO, BEN, FAR FROM IT.
MY WORK HAS JUST STARTED.

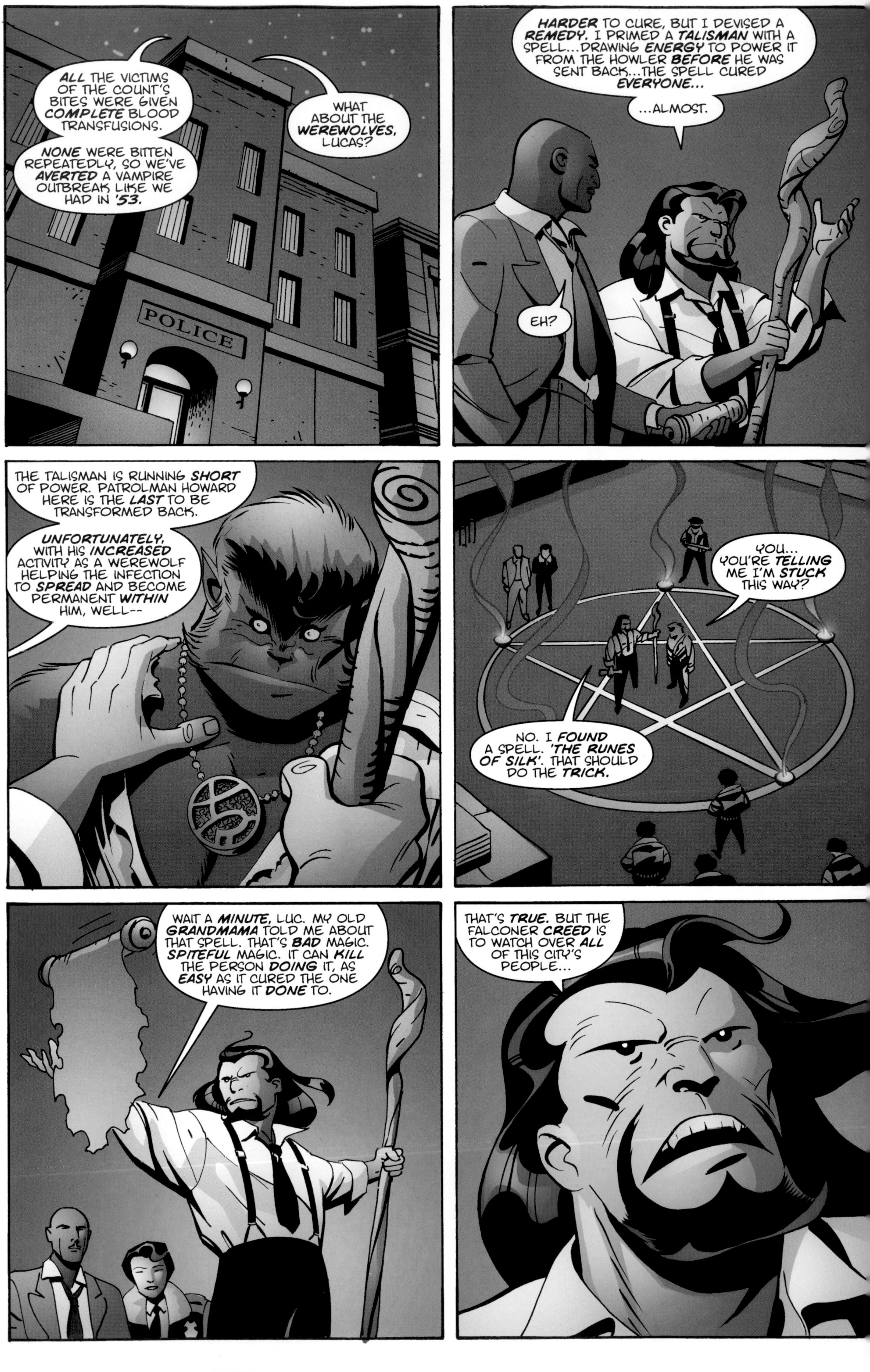
ALL THE VICTIMS OF THE COUNT'S BITES WERE GIVEN COMPLETE BLOOD TRANSFUSIONS.
NONE WERE BITTEN REPEATEDLY, SO WE'VE AVERTED A VAMPIRE OUTBREAK LIKE WE HAD IN '53.
WHAT ABOUT THE WEREWOLVES, LUCAS?
POLICE
HARDER TO CURE, BUT I DEVISED A REMEDY. I PRIMED A TALISMAN WITH A SPELL...DRAWING ENERGY TO POWER IT FROM THE HOWLER BEFORE HE WAS SENT BACK...THE SPELL CURED EVERYONE...
...ALMOST.
EH?
THE TALISMAN IS RUNNING SHORT OF POWER. PATROLMAN HOWARD HERE IS THE LAST TO BE TRANSFORMED BACK.
UNFORTUNATELY, WITH HIS INCREASED ACTIVITY AS A WEREWOLF HELPING THE INFECTION TO SPREAD AND BECOME PERMANENT WITHIN HIM, WELL--
YOU... YOU'RE TELLING ME I'M STUCK THIS WAY?
NO. I FOUND A SPELL. 'THE RUNES OF SILK'. THAT SHOULD DO THE TRICK.
WAIT A MINUTE, LUC. MY OLD GRANDMAMA TOLD ME ABOUT THAT SPELL. THAT'S BAD MAGIC. SPITEFUL MAGIC. IT CAN KILL THE PERSON DOING IT, AS EASY AS IT CURED THE ONE HAVING IT DONE TO.
THAT'S TRUE. BUT THE FALCONER CREED IS TO WATCH OVER ALL OF THIS CITY'S PEOPLE...

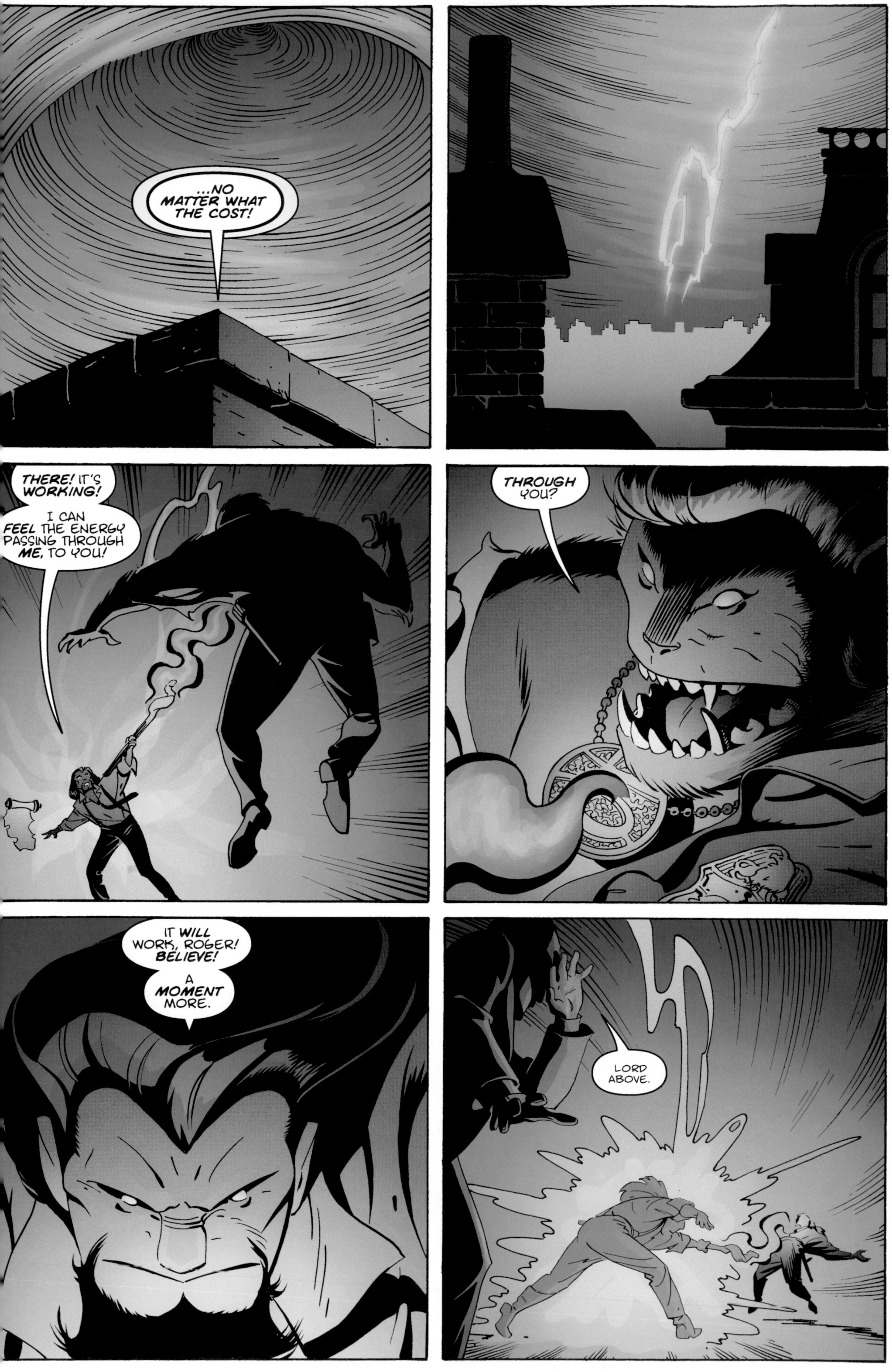
...NO MATTER WHAT THE COST!
THERE! IT'S WORKING!
I CAN FEEL THE ENERGY PASSING THROUGH ME, TO YOU!
THROUGH YOU?
IT WILL WORK, ROGER! BELIEVE!
A MOMENT MORE.
LORD ABOVE.

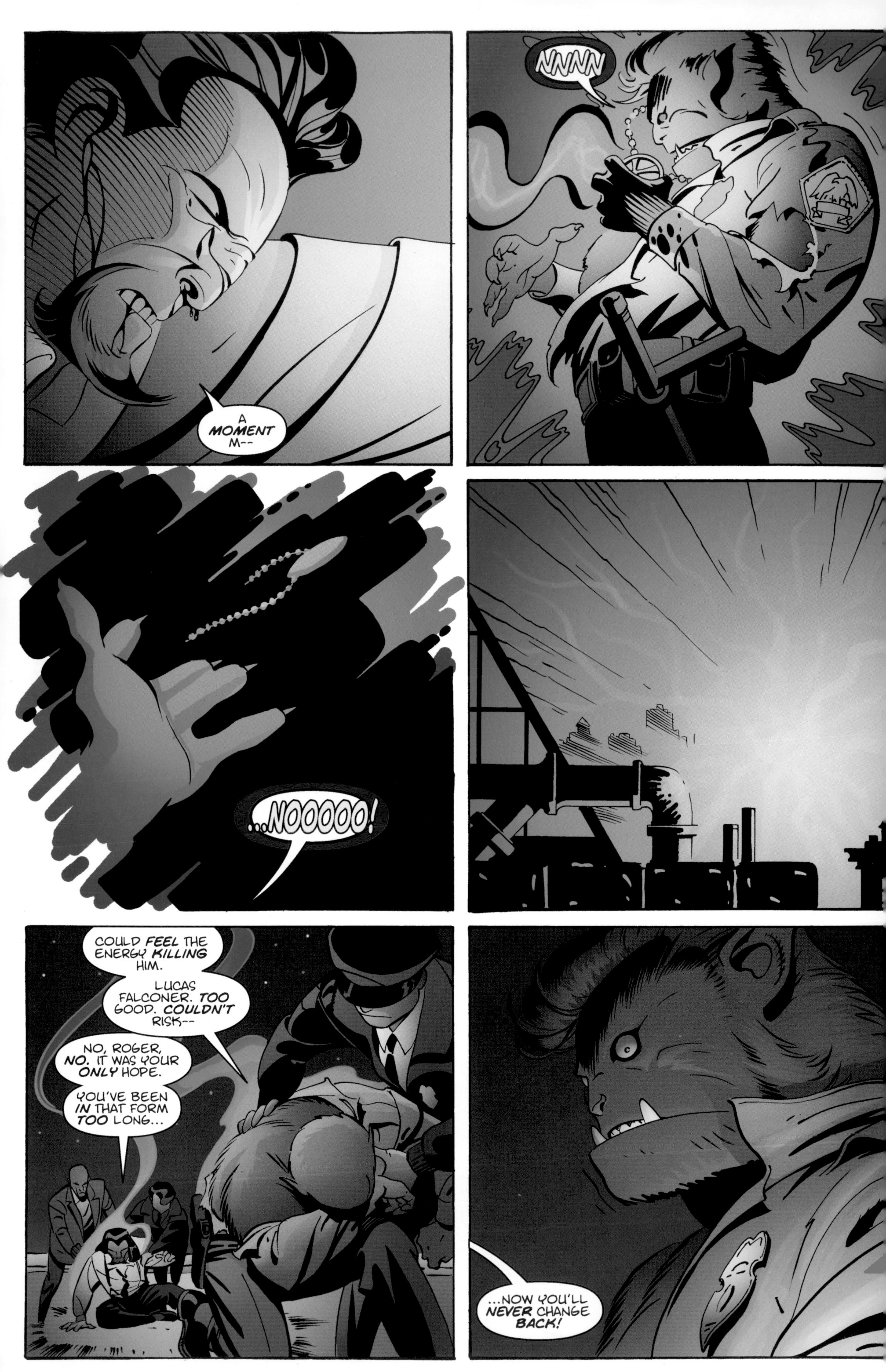
A MOMENT M--
NNNN
...NOOOOO!
COULD FEEL THE ENERGY KILLING HIM.
LUCAS FALCONER. TOO GOOD. COULDN'T RISK--
NO, ROGER, NO. IT WAS YOUR ONLY HOPE.
YOU'VE BEEN IN THAT FORM TOO LONG...
...NOW YOU'LL NEVER CHANGE BACK!

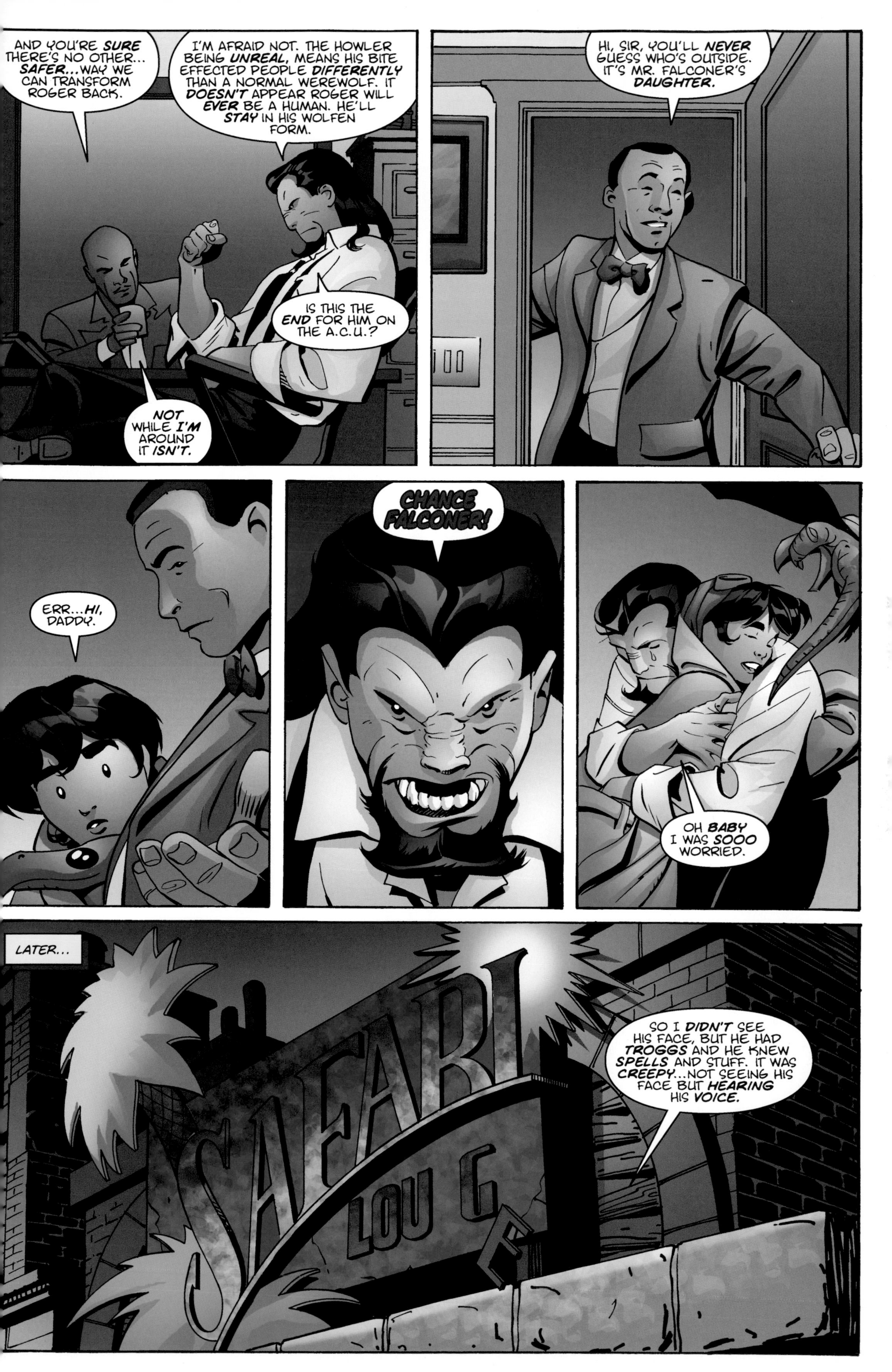
AND YOU'RE SURE THERE'S NO OTHER... SAFER...WAY WE CAN TRANSFORM ROGER BACK.
I'M AFRAID NOT. THE HOWLER BEING UNREAL, MEANS HIS BITE EFFECTED PEOPLE DIFFERENTLY THAN A NORMAL WEREWOLF. IT DOESN'T APPEAR ROGER WILL EVER BE A HUMAN. HE'LL STAY IN HIS WOLFEN FORM.
IS THIS THE END FOR HIM ON THE A.C.U.?
NOT WHILE I'M AROUND IT ISN'T.
HI, SIR, YOU'LL NEVER GUESS WHO'S OUTSIDE. IT'S MR. FALCONER'S DAUGHTER.
ERR...HI, DADDY.
CHANCE FALCONER!
OH BABY I WAS SOOO WORRIED.
LATER...
SAFARI
LOU G
SO I DIDN'T SEE HIS FACE, BUT HE HAD TROGGS AND HE KNEW SPELLS AND STUFF. IT WAS CREEPY...NOT SEEING HIS FACE BUT HEARING HIS VOICE.

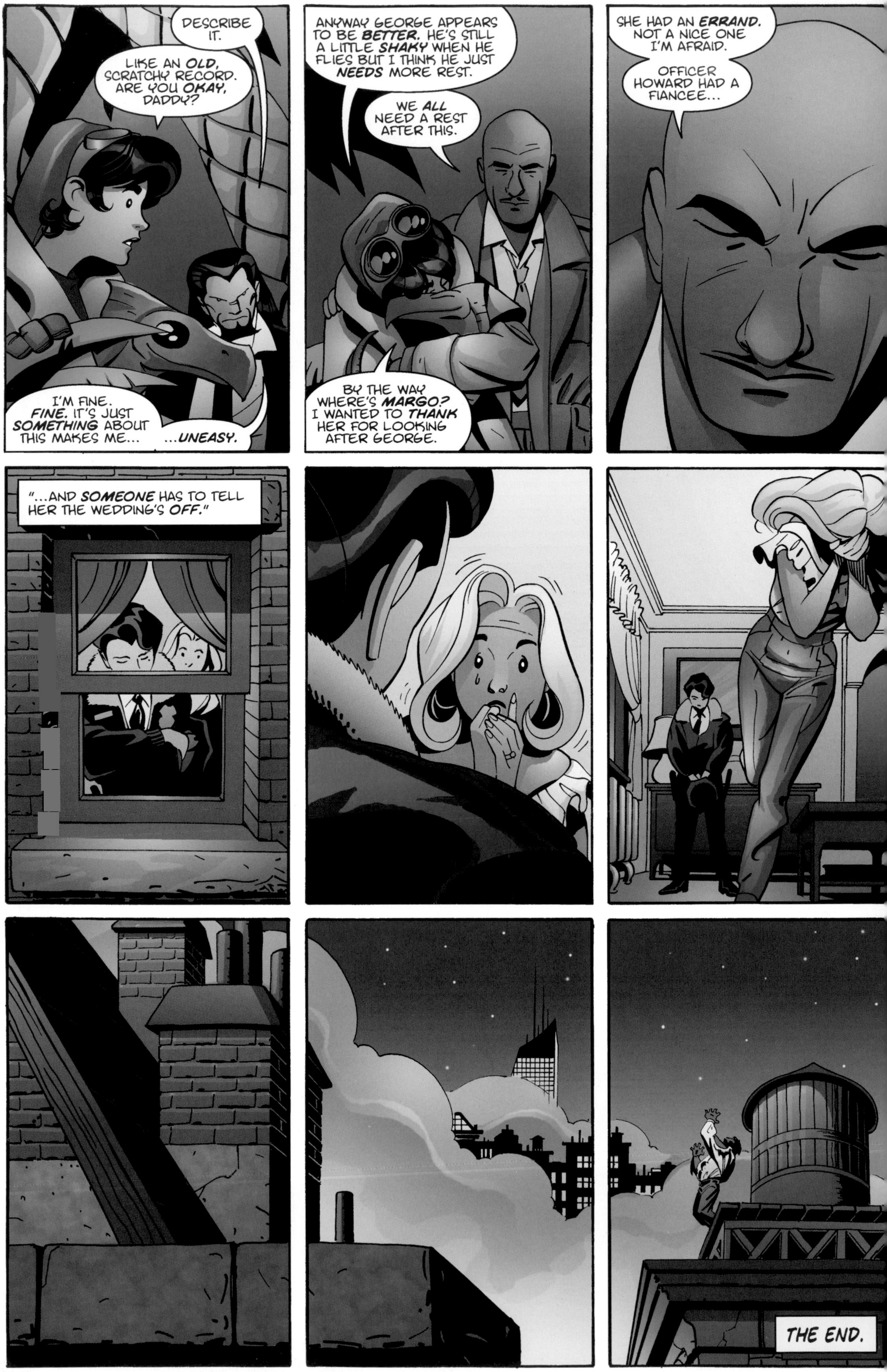

DESCRIBE IT.
LIKE AN OLD, SCRATCHY RECORD. ARE YOU OKAY, DADDY?
I'M FINE. FINE. IT'S JUST SOMETHING ABOUT THIS MAKES ME...
...UNEASY.
ANYWAY GEORGE APPEARS TO BE BETTER. HE'S STILL A LITTLE SHAKY WHEN HE FLIES BUT I THINK HE JUST NEEDS MORE REST.
WE ALL NEED A REST AFTER THIS.
BY THE WAY WHERE'S MARGO? I WANTED TO THANK HER FOR LOOKING AFTER GEORGE.
SHE HAD AN ERRAND. NOT A NICE ONE I'M AFRAID.
OFFICER HOWARD HAD A FIANCEE...
"...AND SOMEONE HAS TO TELL HER THE WEDDING'S OFF."
THE END.

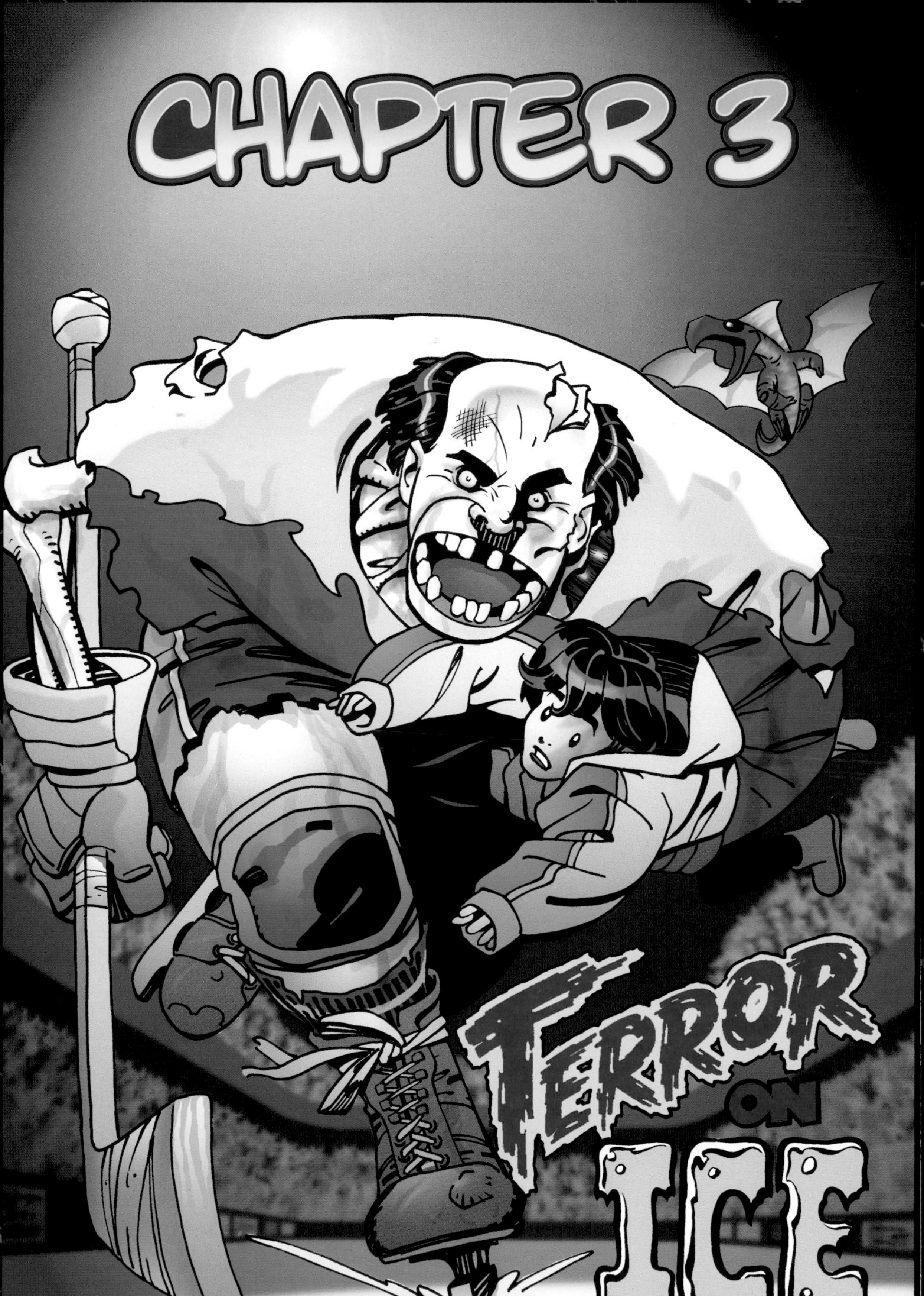
CHAPTER 3
TERROR ON ICE

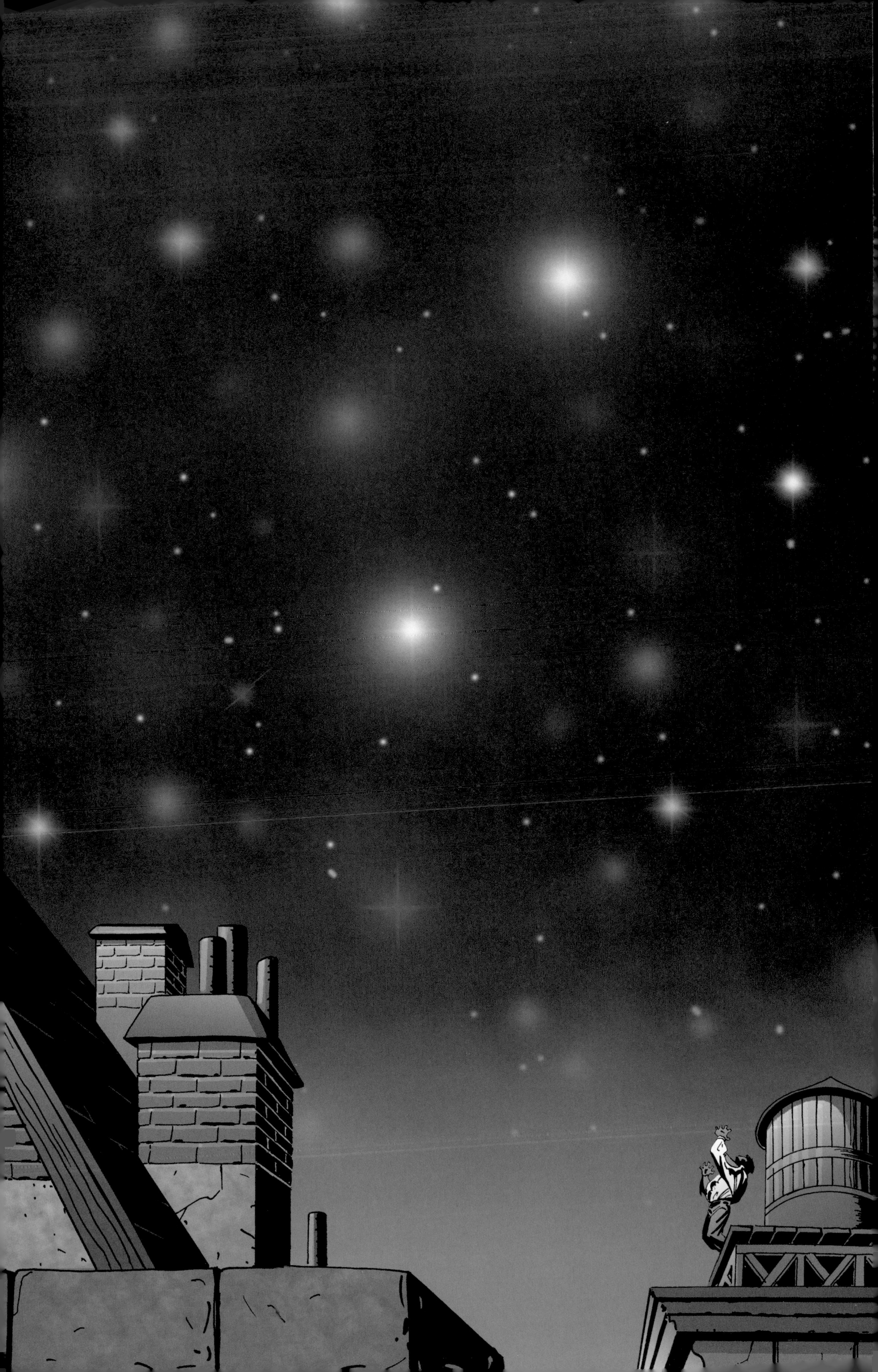

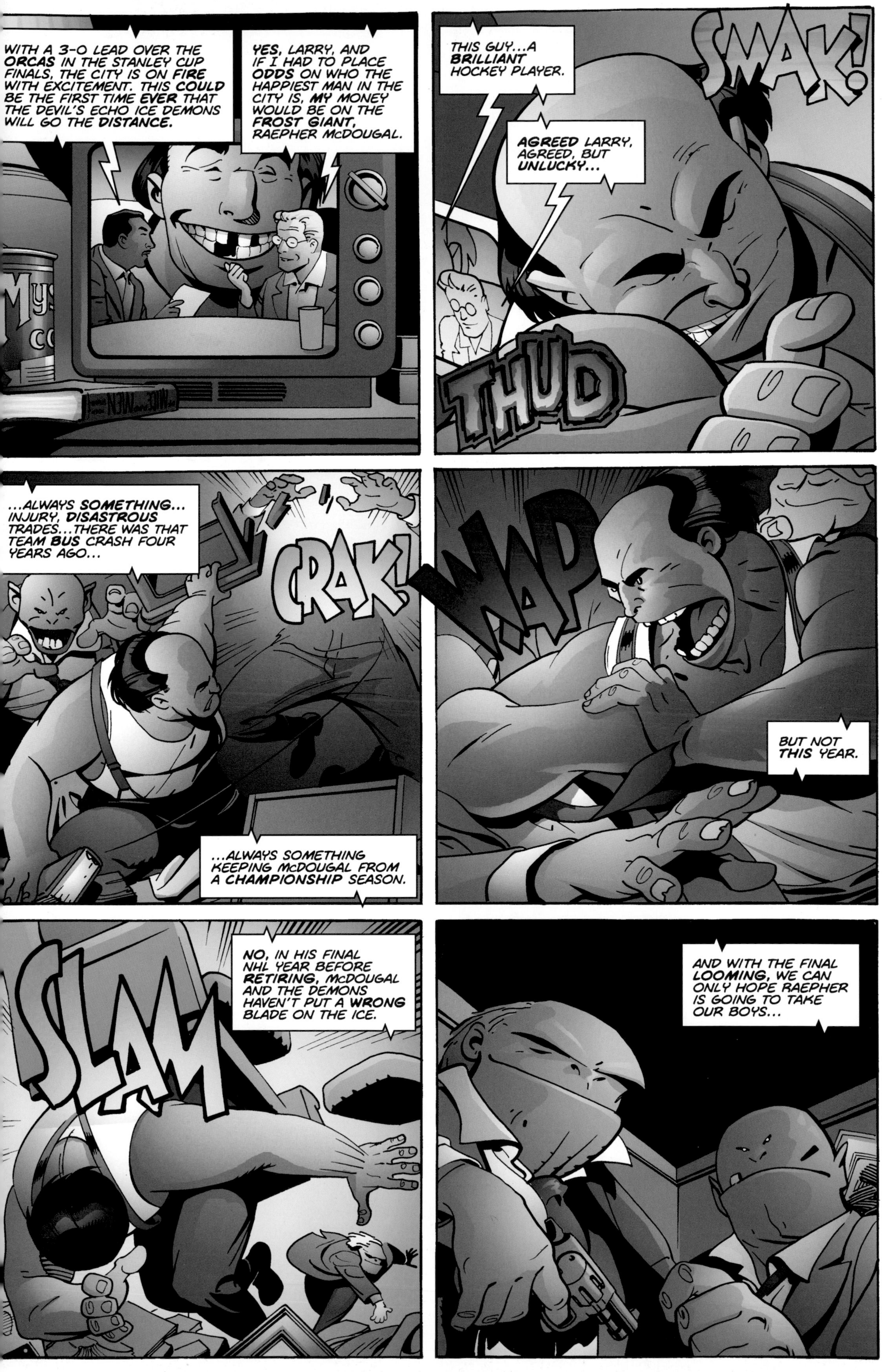
WITH A 3-0 LEAD OVER THE ORCAS IN THE STANLEY CUP FINALS, THE CITY IS ON FIRE WITH EXCITEMENT. THIS COULD BE THE FIRST TIME EVER THAT THE DEVIL'S ECHO ICE DEMONS WILL GO THE DISTANCE.
YES, LARRY, AND IF I HAD TO PLACE ODDS ON WHO THE HAPPIEST MAN IN THE CITY IS, MY MONEY WOULD BE ON THE FROST GIANT, RAEPHER McDOUGAL.
SMAK!
THIS GUY...A BRILLIANT HOCKEY PLAYER.
AGREED LARRY, AGREED, BUT UNLUCKY...
THUD
...ALWAYS SOMETHING... INJURY, DISASTROUS TRADES...THERE WAS THAT TEAM BUS CRASH FOUR YEARS AGO...
CRAK!
...ALWAYS SOMETHING KEEPING McDOUGAL FROM A CHAMPIONSHIP SEASON.
WAP
BUT NOT THIS YEAR.
SLAM
NO, IN HIS FINAL NHL YEAR BEFORE RETIRING, McDOUGAL AND THE DEMONS HAVEN'T PUT A WRONG BLADE ON THE ICE.
AND WITH THE FINAL LOOMING, WE CAN ONLY HOPE RAEPHER IS GOING TO TAKE OUR BOYS...

ALL THE WAY!
BLAM
BLAM
BLAM
ROBINSON & SMITH
DEAD MEN CAN'T SKATE
GEORGE FREEMAN
INKS
JEROMY COX
COLOR
AMIE GRENIER
LETTERING
JOHN LAYMAN
EDITOR

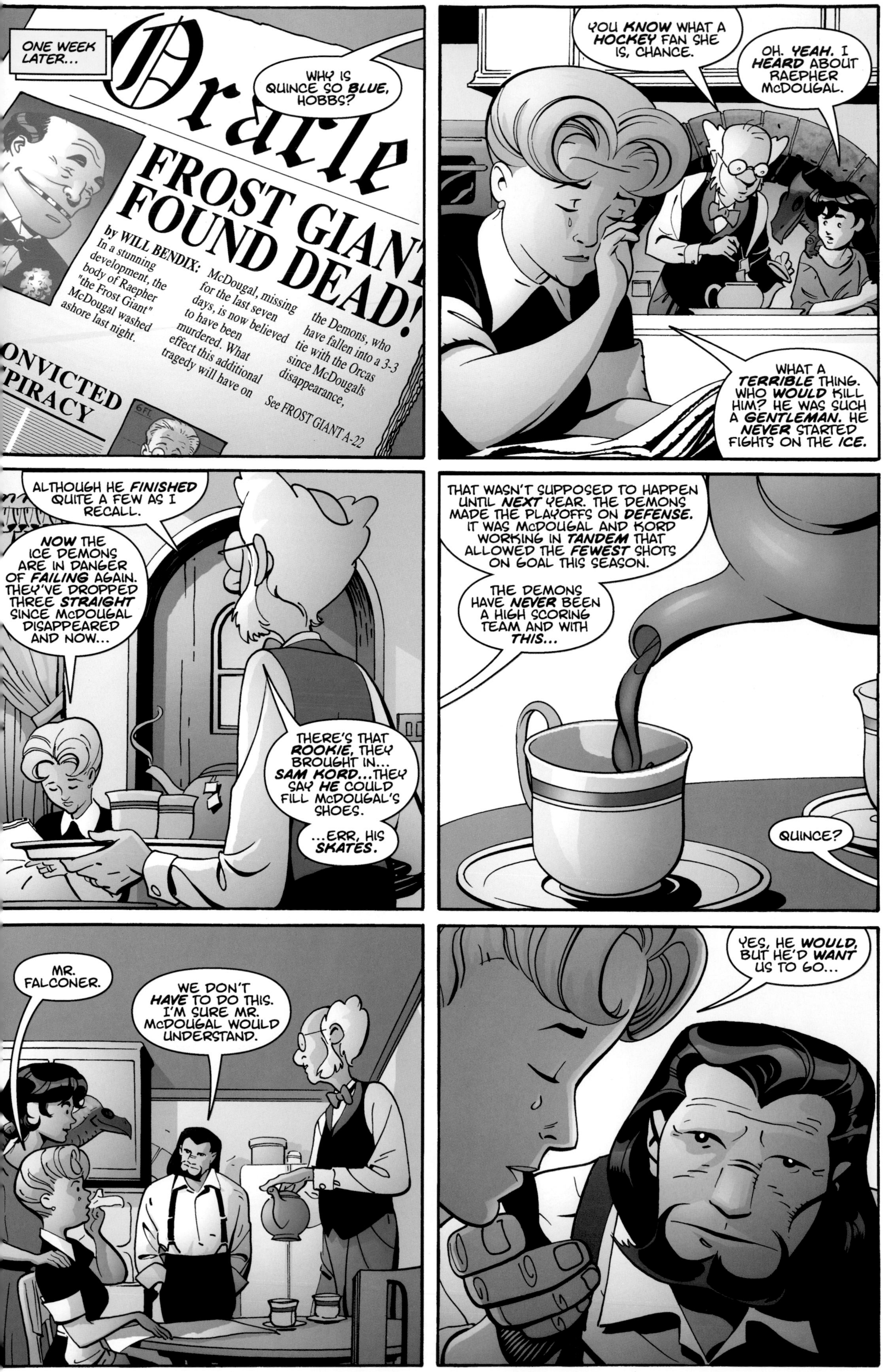
ONE WEEK LATER...
Oracle
FROST GIANT FOUND DEAD!
by WILL BENDIX: In a stunning development, the body of Raepher McDougal "the Frost Giant" McDougal washed ashore last night.
McDougal, missing for the last seven days, is now believed to have been murdered. What effect this additional tragedy will have on
the Demons, who have fallen into a 3-3 tie with the Orcas since McDougal's disappearance,
See FROST GIANT A-22
ONVICTED PIRACY
WHY IS QUINCE SO BLUE, HOBBS?
YOU KNOW WHAT A HOCKEY FAN SHE IS, CHANCE.
OH. YEAH. I HEARD ABOUT RAEPHER McDOUGAL.
WHAT A TERRIBLE THING. WHO WOULD KILL HIM? HE WAS SUCH A GENTLEMAN. HE NEVER STARTED FIGHTS ON THE ICE.
ALTHOUGH HE FINISHED QUITE A FEW AS I RECALL.
NOW THE ICE DEMONS ARE IN DANGER OF FAILING AGAIN. THEY'VE DROPPED THREE STRAIGHT SINCE McDOUGAL DISAPPEARED AND NOW...
THERE'S THAT ROOKIE, THEY BROUGHT IN... SAM KORD...THEY SAY HE COULD FILL McDOUGAL'S SHOES.
...ERR, HIS SKATES.
THAT WASN'T SUPPOSED TO HAPPEN UNTIL NEXT YEAR. THE DEMONS MADE THE PLAYOFFS ON DEFENSE. IT WAS McDOUGAL AND KORD WORKING IN TANDEM THAT ALLOWED THE FEWEST SHOTS ON GOAL THIS SEASON.
THE DEMONS HAVE NEVER BEEN A HIGH SCORING TEAM AND WITH THIS...
QUINCE?
MR. FALCONER.
WE DON'T HAVE TO DO THIS. I'M SURE MR. McDOUGAL WOULD UNDERSTAND.
YES, HE WOULD, BUT HE'D WANT US TO GO...

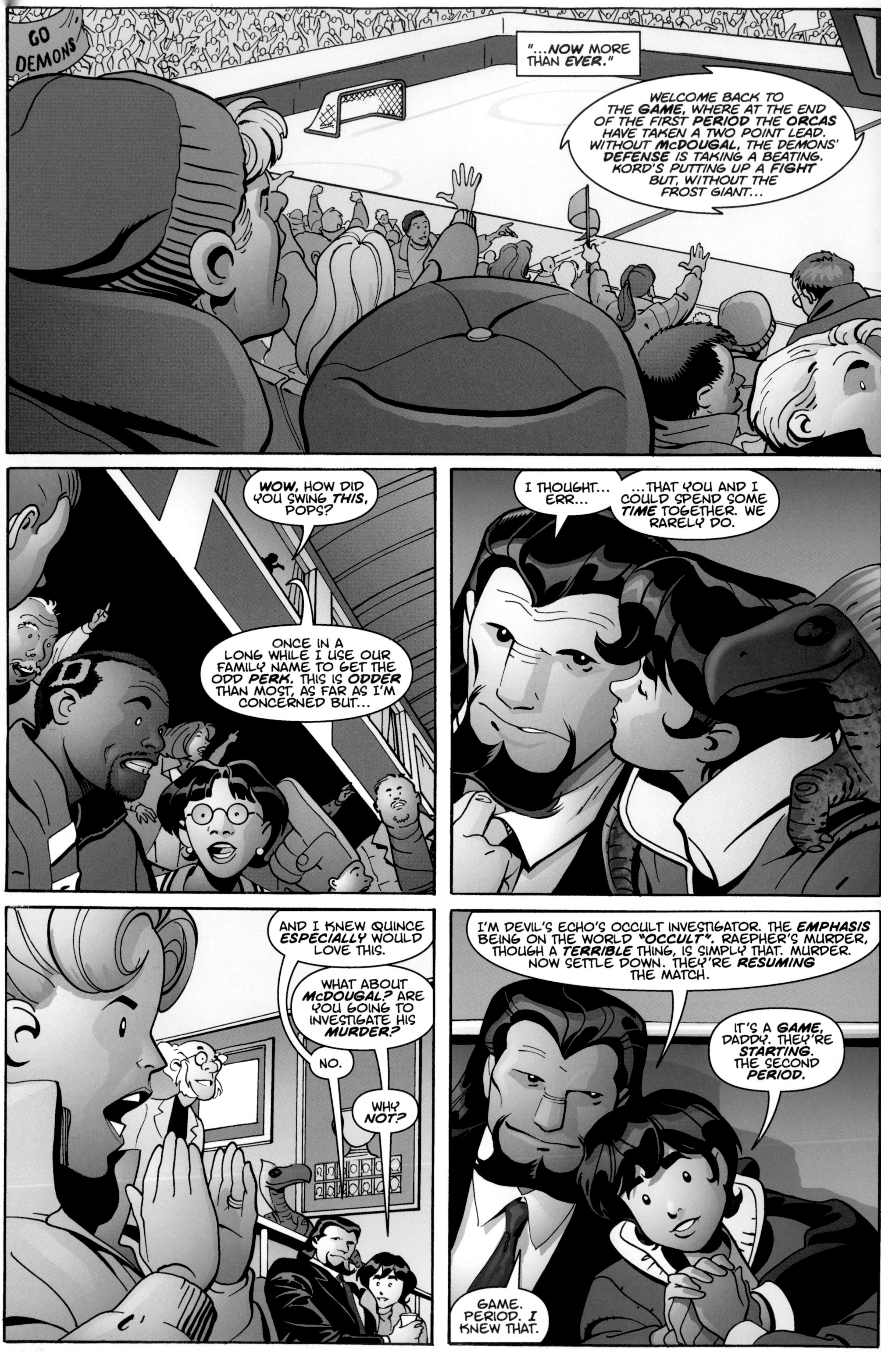
GO DEMONS
"...NOW MORE THAN EVER."
WELCOME BACK TO THE GAME, WHERE AT THE END OF THE FIRST PERIOD THE ORCAS HAVE TAKEN A TWO POINT LEAD. WITHOUT McDOUGAL, THE DEMONS' DEFENSE IS TAKING A BEATING. KORD'S PUTTING UP A FIGHT BUT, WITHOUT THE FROST GIANT...
WOW, HOW DID YOU SWING THIS, POPS?
ONCE IN A LONG WHILE I USE OUR FAMILY NAME TO GET THE ODD PERK. THIS IS ODDER THAN MOST, AS FAR AS I'M CONCERNED BUT...
I THOUGHT... ERR...
...THAT YOU AND I COULD SPEND SOME TIME TOGETHER. WE RARELY DO.
AND I KNEW QUINCE ESPECIALLY WOULD LOVE THIS.
WHAT ABOUT McDOUGAL? ARE YOU GOING TO INVESTIGATE HIS MURDER?
NO.
WHY NOT?
I'M DEVIL'S ECHO'S OCCULT INVESTIGATOR. THE EMPHASIS BEING ON THE WORLD "OCCULT". RAEPHER'S MURDER, THOUGH A TERRIBLE THING, IS SIMPLY THAT. MURDER. NOW SETTLE DOWN. THEY'RE RESUMING THE MATCH.
IT'S A GAME, DADDY. THEY'RE STARTING. THE SECOND PERIOD.
GAME. PERIOD. I KNEW THAT.

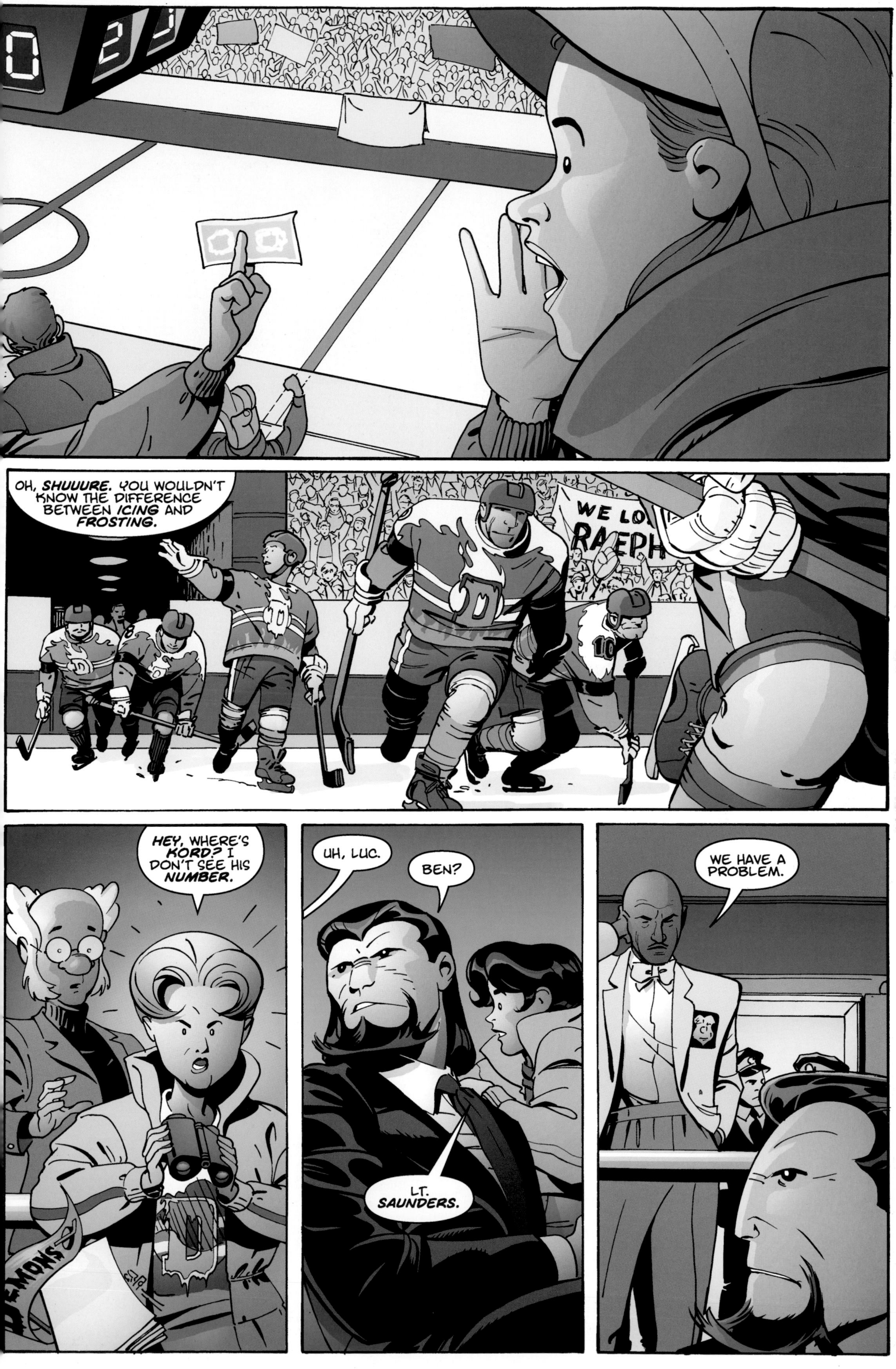

OH, SHUUURE. YOU WOULDN'T KNOW THE DIFFERENCE BETWEEN ICING AND FROSTING.
WE LO
RALPH
HEY, WHERE'S KORD? I DON'T SEE HIS NUMBER.
DEMONS
UH, LUC.
BEN?
LT. SAUNDERS.
WE HAVE A PROBLEM.

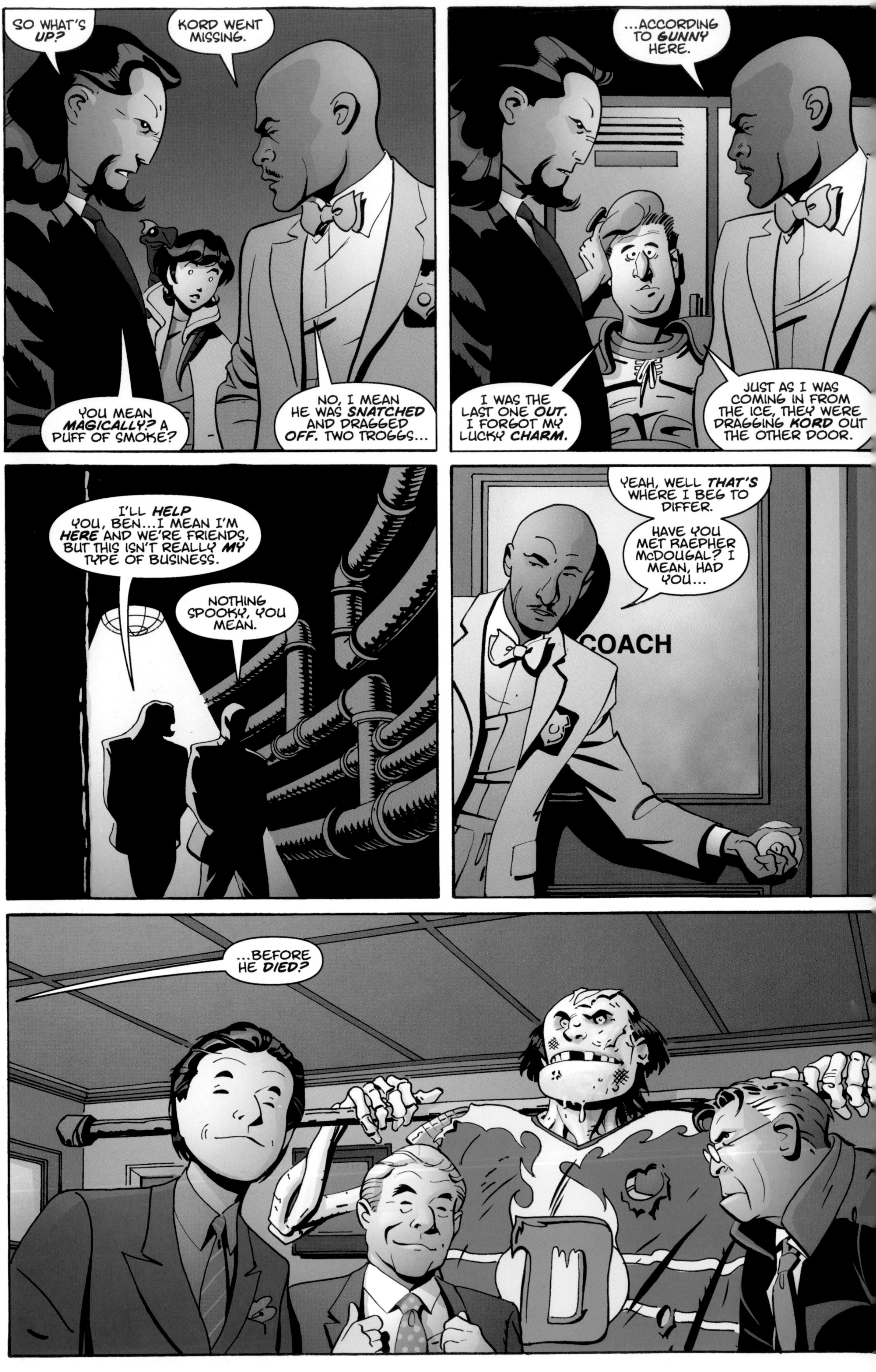
SO WHAT'S UP?
KORD WENT MISSING.
YOU MEAN MAGICALLY? A PUFF OF SMOKE?
NO, I MEAN HE WAS SNATCHED AND DRAGGED OFF. TWO TROGGS...
...ACCORDING TO GUNNY HERE.
I WAS THE LAST ONE OUT. I FORGOT MY LUCKY CHARM.
JUST AS I WAS COMING IN FROM THE ICE, THEY WERE DRAGGING KORD OUT THE OTHER DOOR.
I'LL HELP YOU, BEN...I MEAN I'M HERE AND WE'RE FRIENDS, BUT THIS ISN'T REALLY MY TYPE OF BUSINESS.
NOTHING SPOOKY, YOU MEAN.
YEAH, WELL THAT'S WHERE I BEG TO DIFFER.
HAVE YOU MET RAEPHER McDOUGAL? I MEAN, HAD YOU...
COACH
...BEFORE HE DIED?

IT'S ALL *RELATIVE.* ALIVE OR DEAD. IT'S LIKE *HOCKEY.* ON THE ICE OR IN THE PENALTY BOX, I'M *STILL* A HOCKEY PLAYER.

HOW DID YOU *GET* HERE?

I DUNNO. I KNOW I WANTED TO PLAY THE FINALS WITH ALL MY *SOUL...* AND THAT BROUGHT ME BACK *HERE.*

WHO *KILLED* YOU RAEPHER, DO YOU RECALL?

TROGGS. TWO OV'EM. I'D NEVER SEEN A *TROGG* BEFORE THAT. I DIDN'T RECOGNIZE THEM...

...ALTHOUGH I WOULD IF I SAW THEM *AGAIN.*

THERE'S NO *WAY* McDOUGAL'S PLAYING.

WHO'S THIS?

JOHN WILBY, THE ORCAS' MANAGER.

JUST *TRY* TO STOP US FROM PUTTING HIM ON THE ICE, WILBY.

...AND DANIEL FARINO, THE DEMON'S *OWNER,* I'M SURE YOU KNOW.

HI, I'M JERRY FARINO, IS *SON.* IT'S AN *HONOR* TO MEET YOU, MR. FALCONER. I JUST WISH THE CIRCUMSTANCES WERE LESS--

I'M USED TO IT.

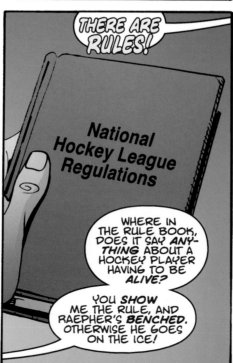

THERE ARE RULES!

National Hockey League Regulations

WHERE IN THE RULE BOOK, DOES IT SAY *ANYTHING* ABOUT A HOCKEY PLAYER HAVING TO BE *ALIVE?*

YOU *SHOW* ME THE RULE, AND RAEPHER'S *BENCHED.* OTHERWISE HE GOES ON THE ICE!

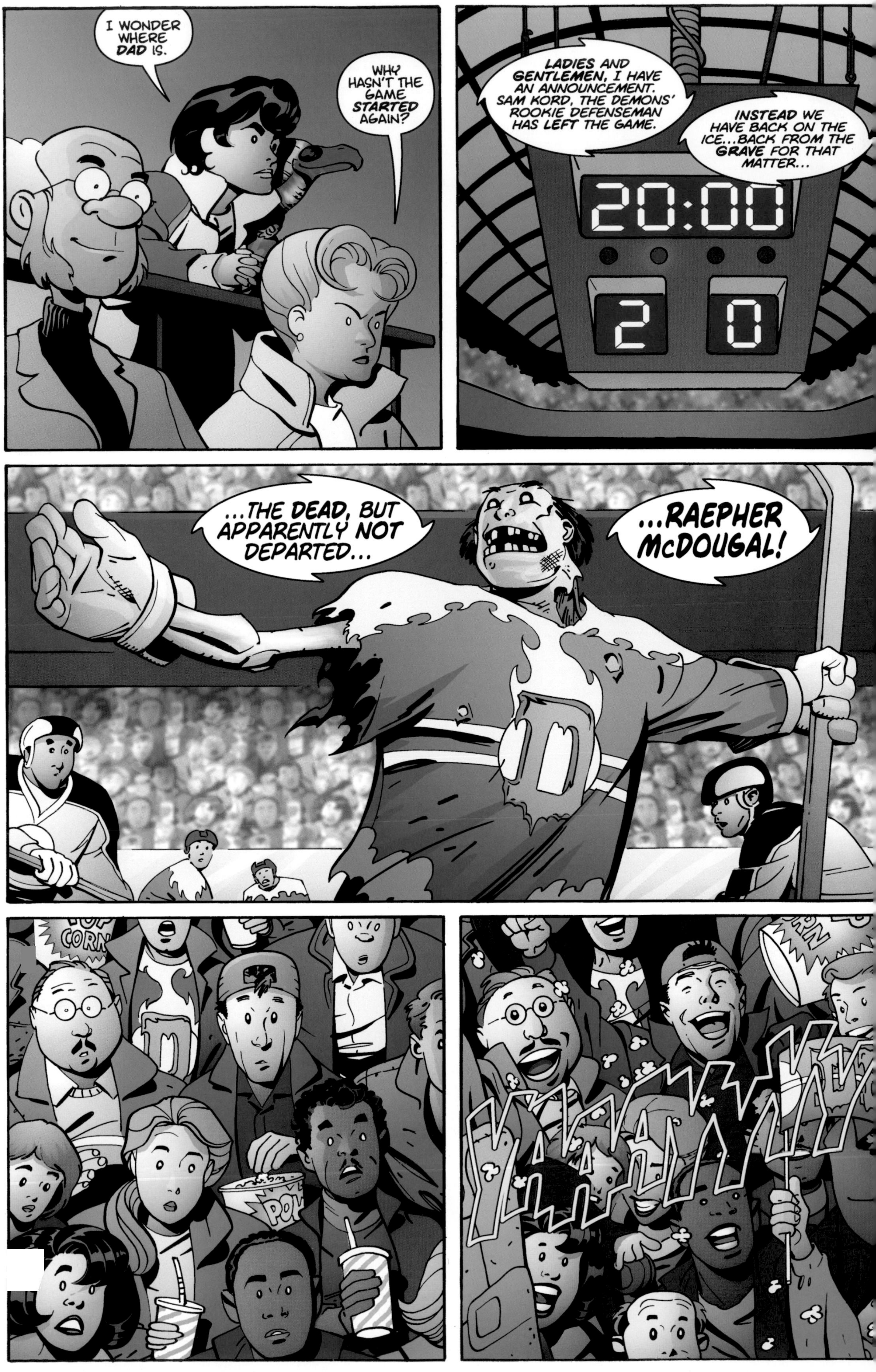
I WONDER WHERE DAD IS.
WHY HASN'T THE GAME STARTED AGAIN?
LADIES AND GENTLEMEN, I HAVE AN ANNOUNCEMENT. SAM KORD, THE DEMONS' ROOKIE DEFENSEMAN HAS LEFT THE GAME.
INSTEAD WE HAVE BACK ON THE ICE...BACK FROM THE GRAVE FOR THAT MATTER...
20:00
2
0
...THE DEAD, BUT APPARENTLY NOT DEPARTED...
...RAEPHER McDOUGAL!
POP CORN
POP

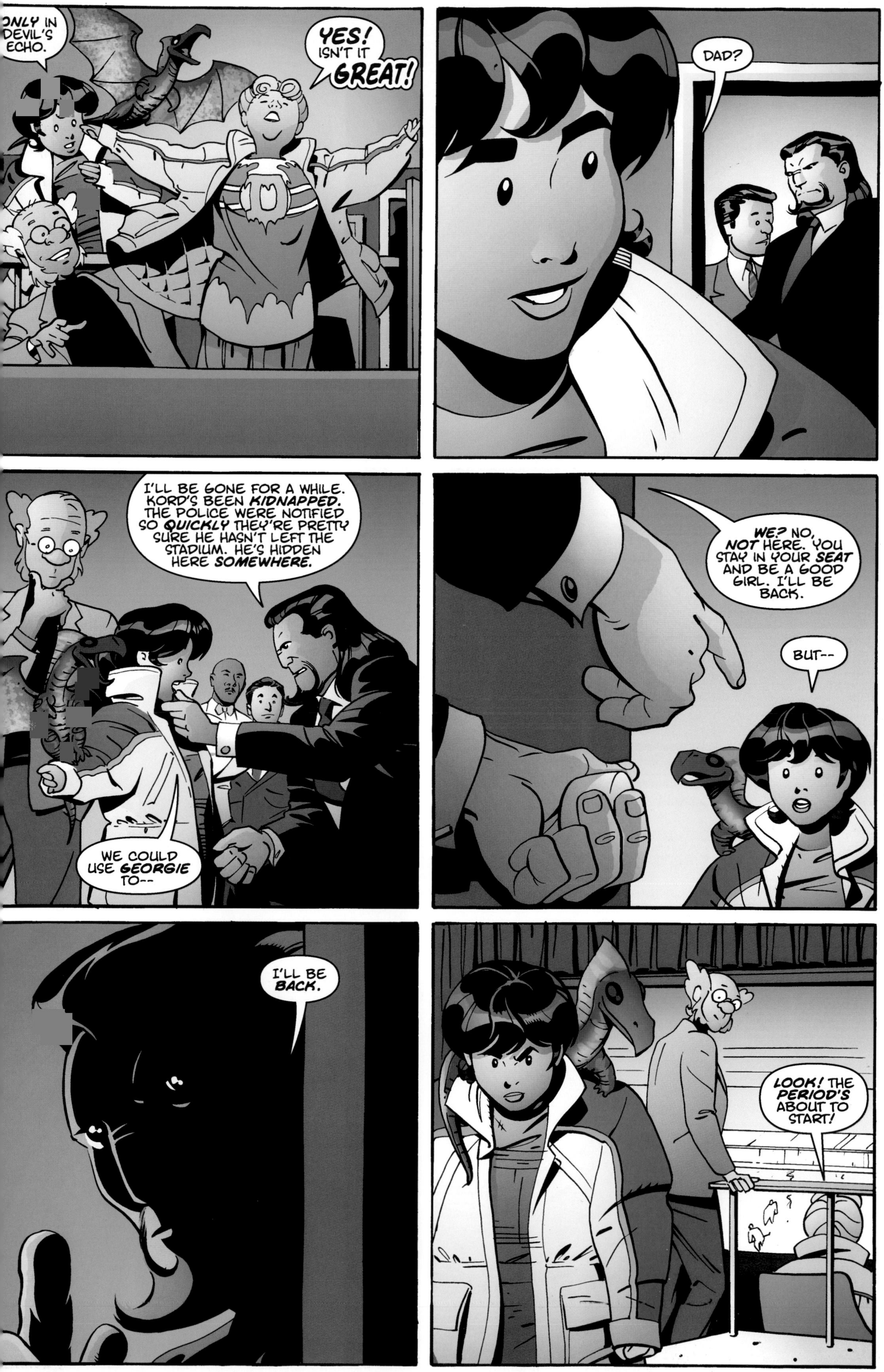
ONLY IN DEVIL'S ECHO.
YES! ISN'T IT GREAT!
DAD?
I'LL BE GONE FOR A WHILE. KORD'S BEEN KIDNAPPED. THE POLICE WERE NOTIFIED SO QUICKLY THEY'RE PRETTY SURE HE HASN'T LEFT THE STADIUM. HE'S HIDDEN HERE SOMEWHERE.
WE COULD USE GEORGIE TO--
WE? NO, NOT HERE. YOU STAY IN YOUR SEAT AND BE A GOOD GIRL. I'LL BE BACK.
BUT--
I'LL BE BACK.
LOOK! THE PERIOD'S ABOUT TO START!

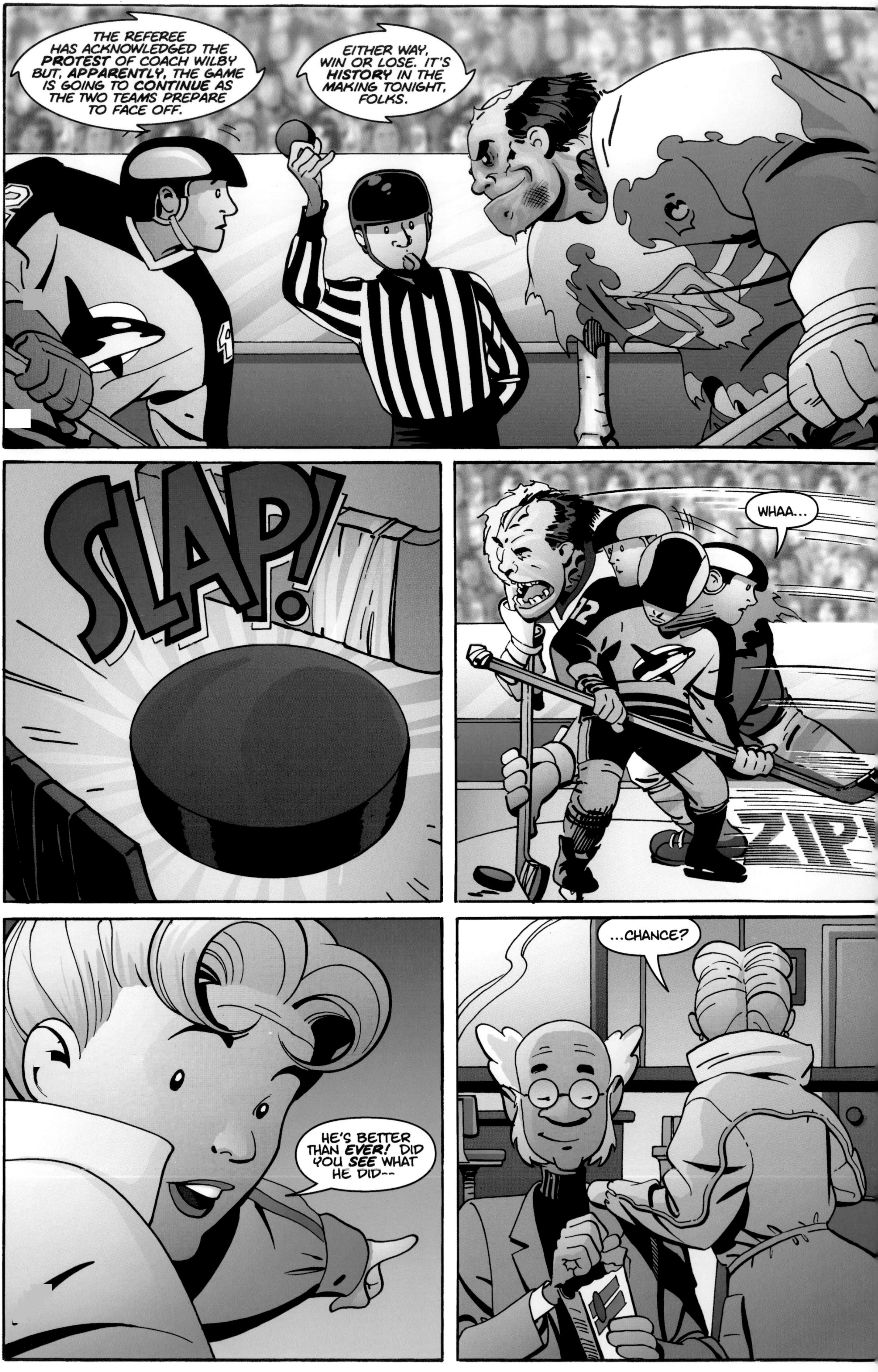
THE REFEREE HAS ACKNOWLEDGED THE PROTEST OF COACH WILBY BUT, APPARENTLY, THE GAME IS GOING TO CONTINUE AS THE TWO TEAMS PREPARE TO FACE OFF.
EITHER WAY, WIN OR LOSE. IT'S HISTORY IN THE MAKING TONIGHT, FOLKS.
SLAP!
WHAA...
ZIP
HE'S BETTER THAN EVER! DID YOU SEE WHAT HE DID--
...CHANCE?

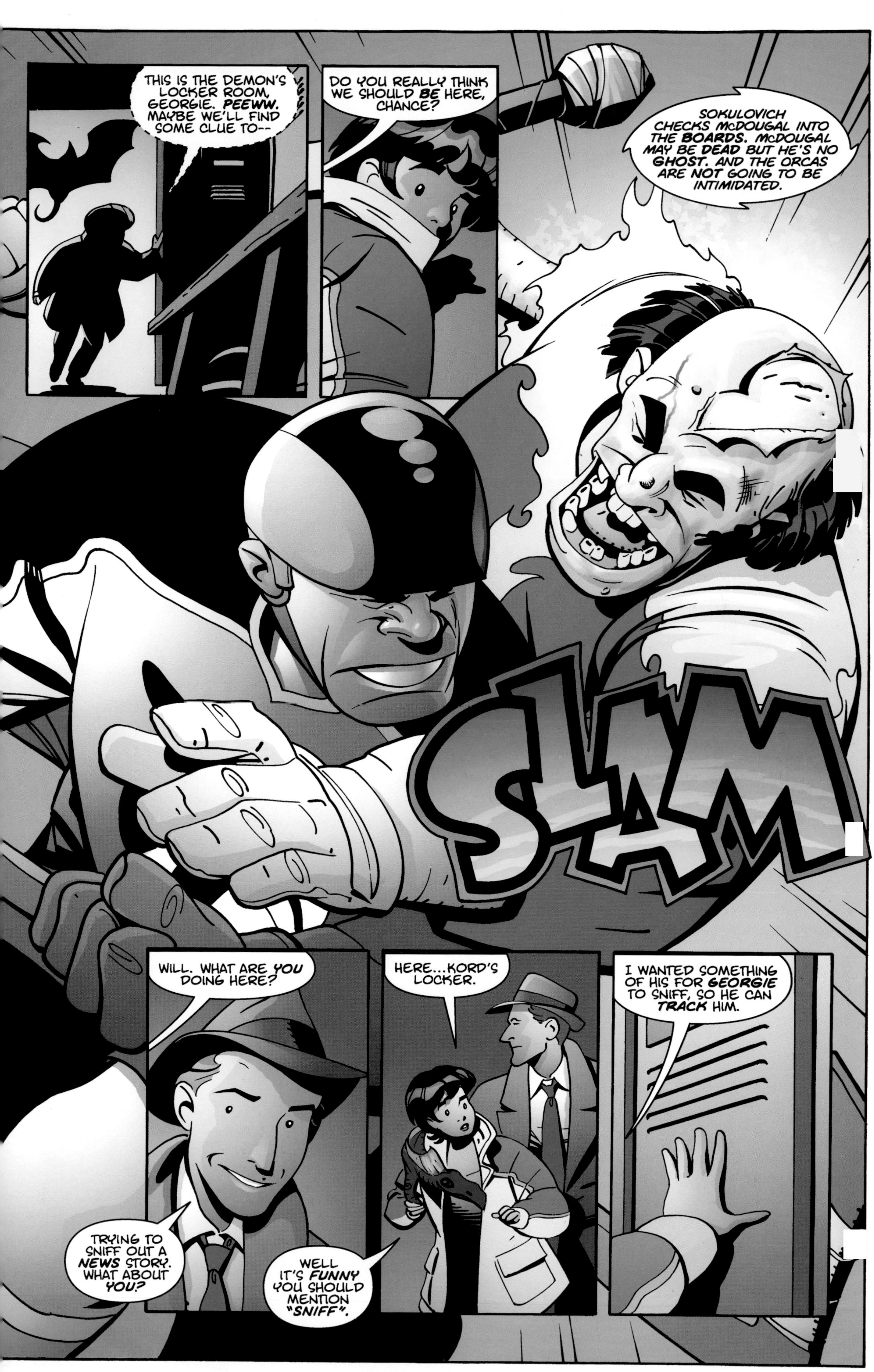
THIS IS THE DEMON'S LOCKER ROOM, GEORGIE. PEEWW. MAYBE WE'LL FIND SOME CLUE TO--
DO YOU REALLY THINK WE SHOULD BE HERE, CHANCE?
SOKULOVICH CHECKS McDOUGAL INTO THE BOARDS. McDOUGAL MAY BE DEAD BUT HE'S NO GHOST. AND THE ORCAS ARE NOT GOING TO BE INTIMIDATED.
SLAM
WILL. WHAT ARE YOU DOING HERE?
TRYING TO SNIFF OUT A NEWS STORY. WHAT ABOUT YOU?
WELL IT'S FUNNY YOU SHOULD MENTION "SNIFF".
HERE...KORD'S LOCKER.
I WANTED SOMETHING OF HIS FOR GEORGIE TO SNIFF, SO HE CAN TRACK HIM.

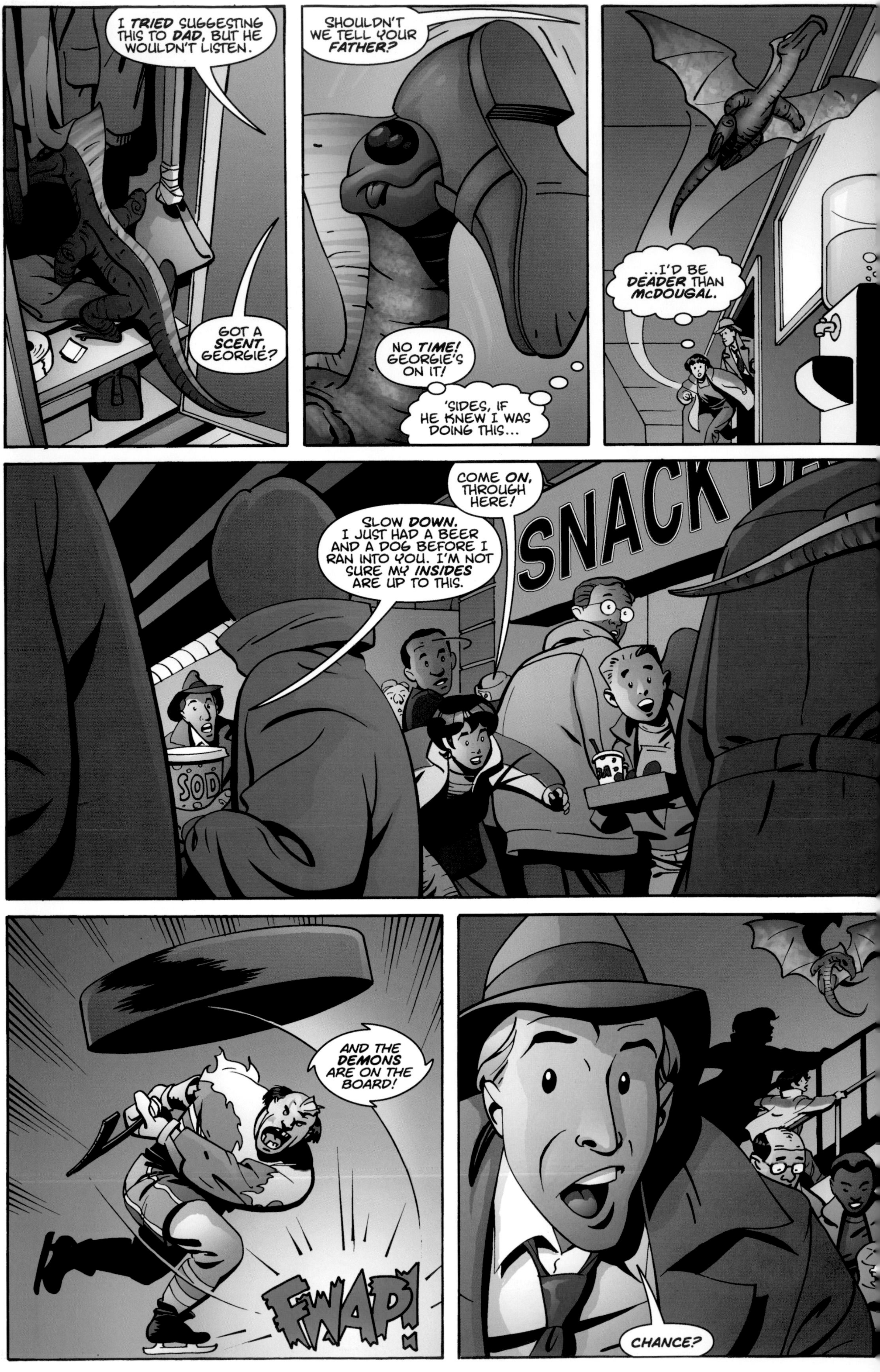
I TRIED SUGGESTING THIS TO DAD, BUT HE WOULDN'T LISTEN.
GOT A SCENT, GEORGIE?
SHOULDN'T WE TELL YOUR FATHER?
NO TIME! GEORGIE'S ON IT!
'SIDES, IF HE KNEW I WAS DOING THIS...
...I'D BE DEADER THAN McDOUGAL.
SNACK
COME ON, THROUGH HERE!
SLOW DOWN. I JUST HAD A BEER AND A DOG BEFORE I RAN INTO YOU. I'M NOT SURE MY INSIDES ARE UP TO THIS.
SOD
AND THE DEMONS ARE ON THE BOARD!
FWAP!
CHANCE?

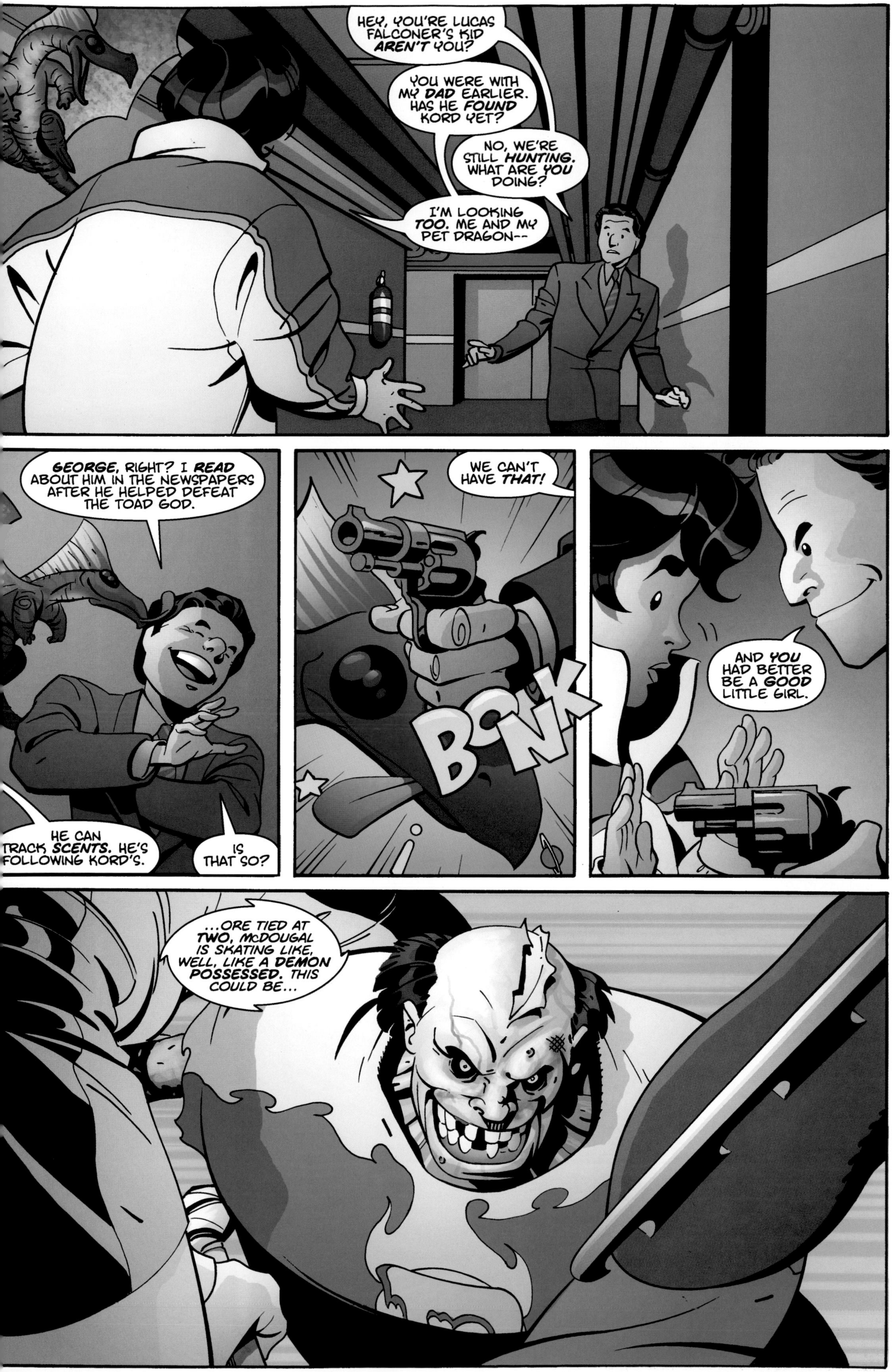
HEY, YOU'RE LUCAS FALCONER'S KID AREN'T YOU?
YOU WERE WITH MY DAD EARLIER. HAS HE FOUND KORD YET?
NO, WE'RE STILL HUNTING. WHAT ARE YOU DOING?
I'M LOOKING TOO. ME AND MY PET DRAGON--
GEORGE, RIGHT? I READ ABOUT HIM IN THE NEWSPAPERS AFTER HE HELPED DEFEAT THE TOAD GOD.
HE CAN TRACK SCENTS. HE'S FOLLOWING KORD'S.
IS THAT SO?
WE CAN'T HAVE THAT!
BONK
AND YOU HAD BETTER BE A GOOD LITTLE GIRL.
...ORE TIED AT TWO, McDOUGAL IS SKATING LIKE, WELL, LIKE A DEMON POSSESSED. THIS COULD BE...

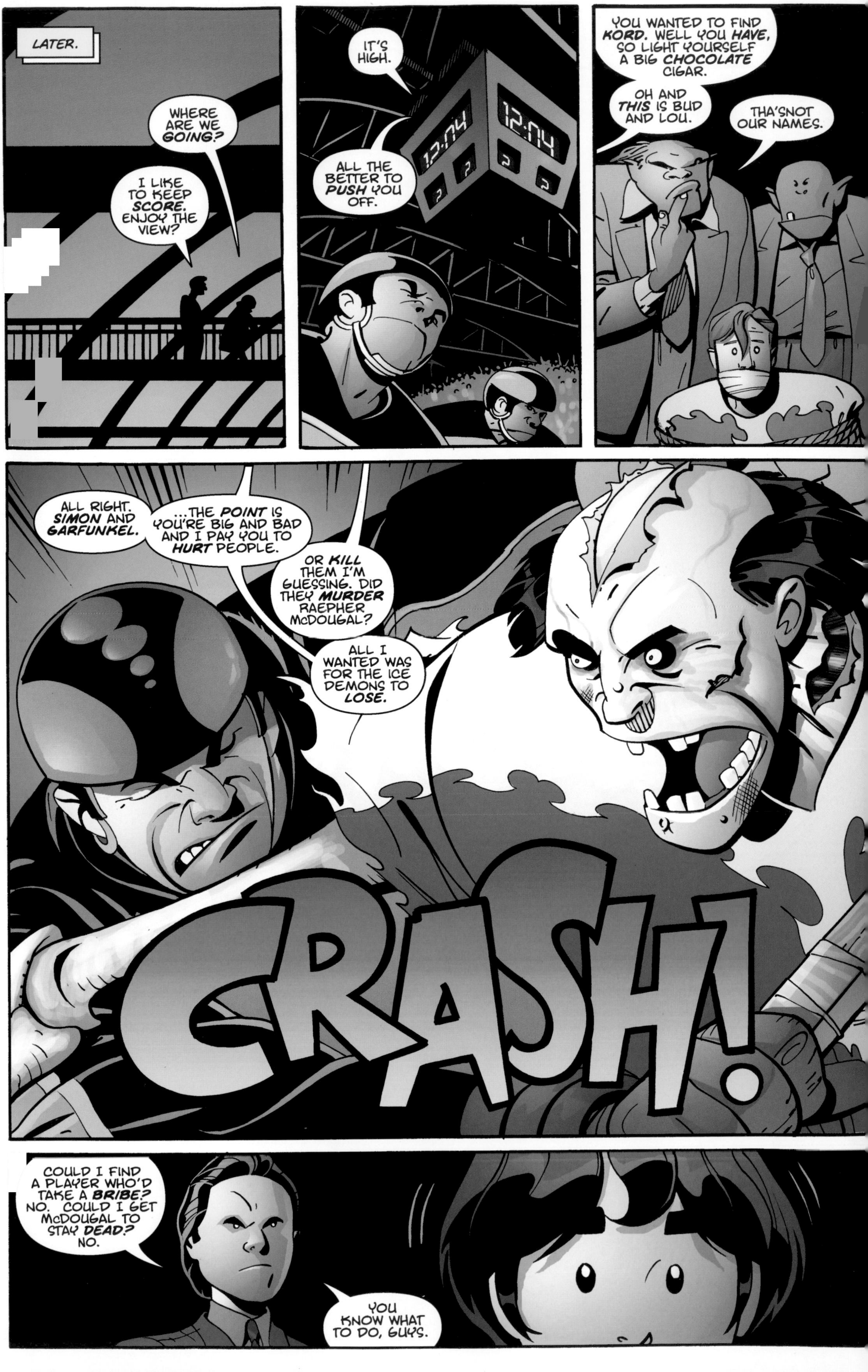
LATER.
WHERE ARE WE GOING?
I LIKE TO KEEP SCORE. ENJOY THE VIEW?
IT'S HIGH.
12:04
12:04
ALL THE BETTER TO PUSH YOU OFF.
YOU WANTED TO FIND KORD. WELL YOU HAVE, SO LIGHT YOURSELF A BIG CHOCOLATE CIGAR.
OH AND THIS IS BUD AND LOU.
THA'SNOT OUR NAMES.
ALL RIGHT. SIMON AND GARFUNKEL.
...THE POINT IS YOU'RE BIG AND BAD AND I PAY YOU TO HURT PEOPLE.
OR KILL THEM I'M GUESSING. DID THEY MURDER RAEPHER McDOUGAL?
ALL I WANTED WAS FOR THE ICE DEMONS TO LOSE.
CRASH!
COULD I FIND A PLAYER WHO'D TAKE A BRIBE? NO. COULD I GET McDOUGAL TO STAY DEAD? NO.
YOU KNOW WHAT TO DO, GUYS.

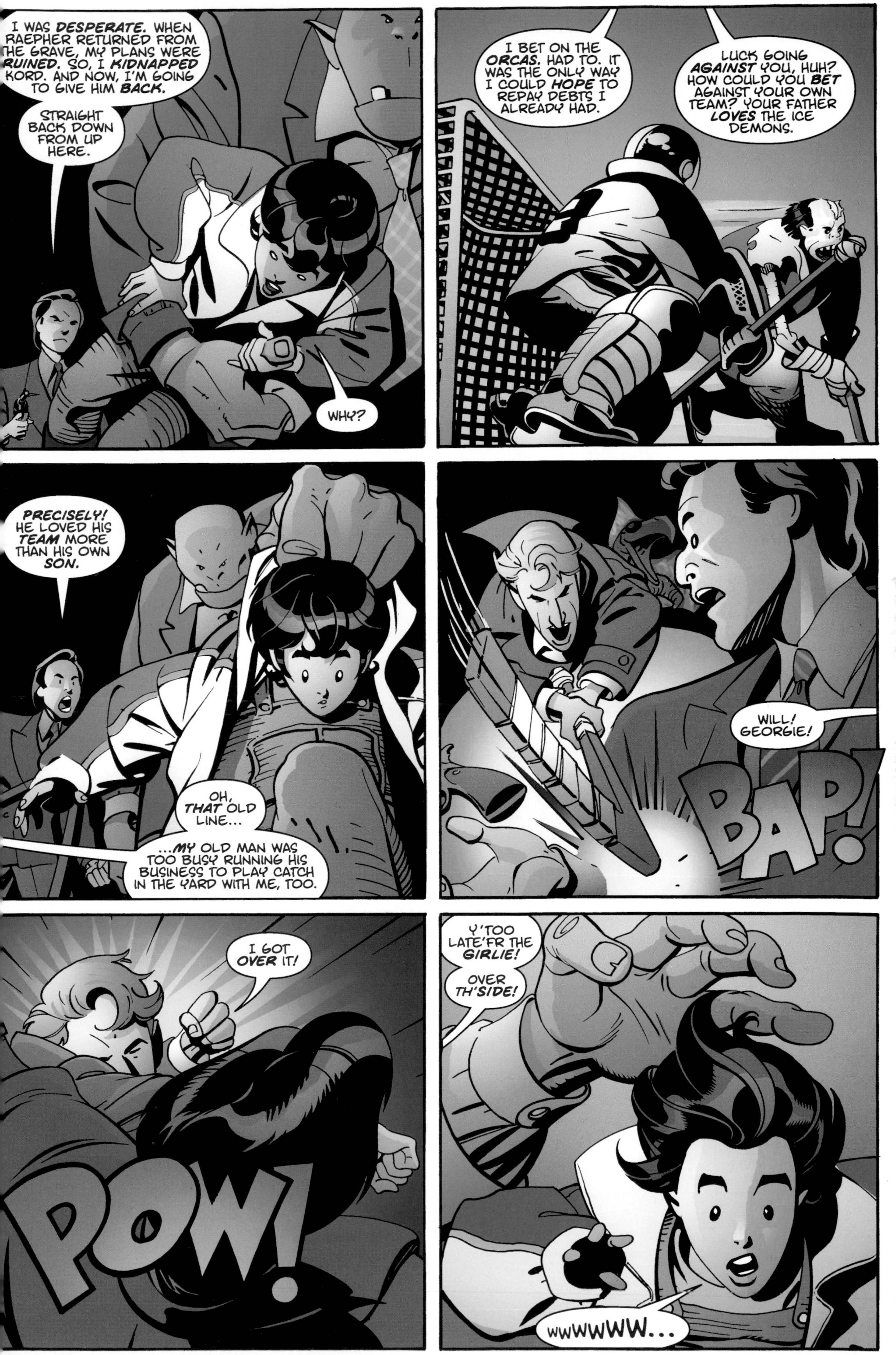
I WAS DESPERATE. WHEN RAEPHER RETURNED FROM THE GRAVE, MY PLANS WERE RUINED. SO, I KIDNAPPED KORD. AND NOW, I'M GOING TO GIVE HIM BACK.
STRAIGHT BACK DOWN FROM UP HERE.
WHY?
I BET ON THE ORCAS. HAD TO. IT WAS THE ONLY WAY I COULD HOPE TO REPAY DEBTS I ALREADY HAD.
LUCK GOING AGAINST YOU, HUH? HOW COULD YOU BET AGAINST YOUR OWN TEAM? YOUR FATHER LOVES THE ICE DEMONS.
PRECISELY! HE LOVED HIS TEAM MORE THAN HIS OWN SON.
OH, THAT OLD LINE...
...MY OLD MAN WAS TOO BUSY RUNNING HIS BUSINESS TO PLAY CATCH IN THE YARD WITH ME, TOO.
WILL! GEORGIE!
BAP!
I GOT OVER IT!
POW!
Y'TOO LATE'FR THE GIRLIE!
OVER TH'SIDE!
WWWWWW...

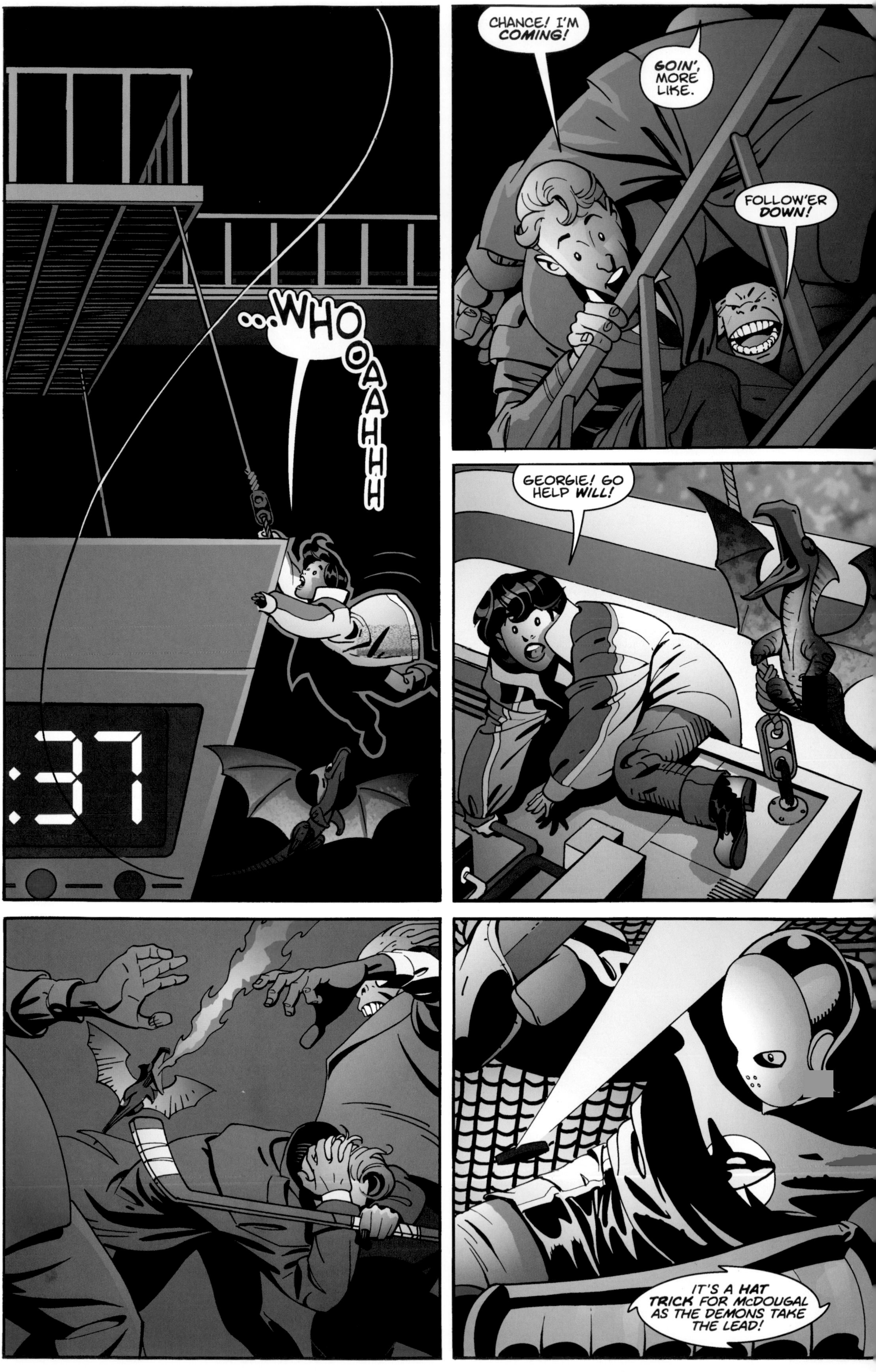

...WHOOAAHHH
:37
CHANCE! I'M COMING!
GOIN', MORE LIKE.
FOLLOW'ER DOWN!
GEORGIE! GO HELP WILL!
IT'S A HAT TRICK FOR McDOUGAL AS THE DEMONS TAKE THE LEAD!

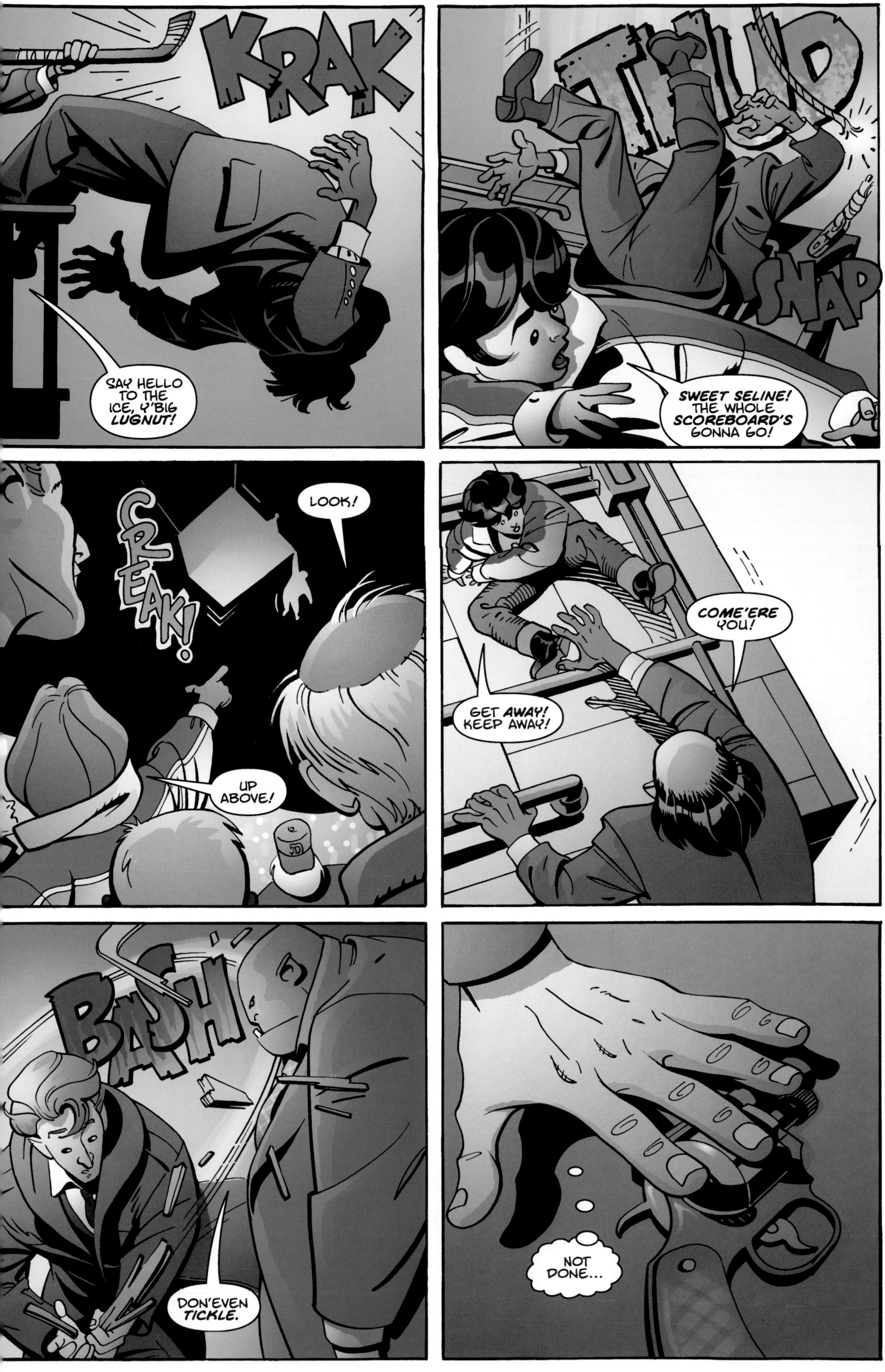
KRAK
SAY HELLO TO THE ICE, Y'BIG LUGNUT!
THUD
SNAP
SWEET SELINE! THE WHOLE SCOREBOARD'S GONNA GO!
CREAK!
LOOK!
UP ABOVE!
COME'ERE YOU!
GET AWAY! KEEP AWAY!
BASH
DON'EVEN TICKLE.
NOT DONE...

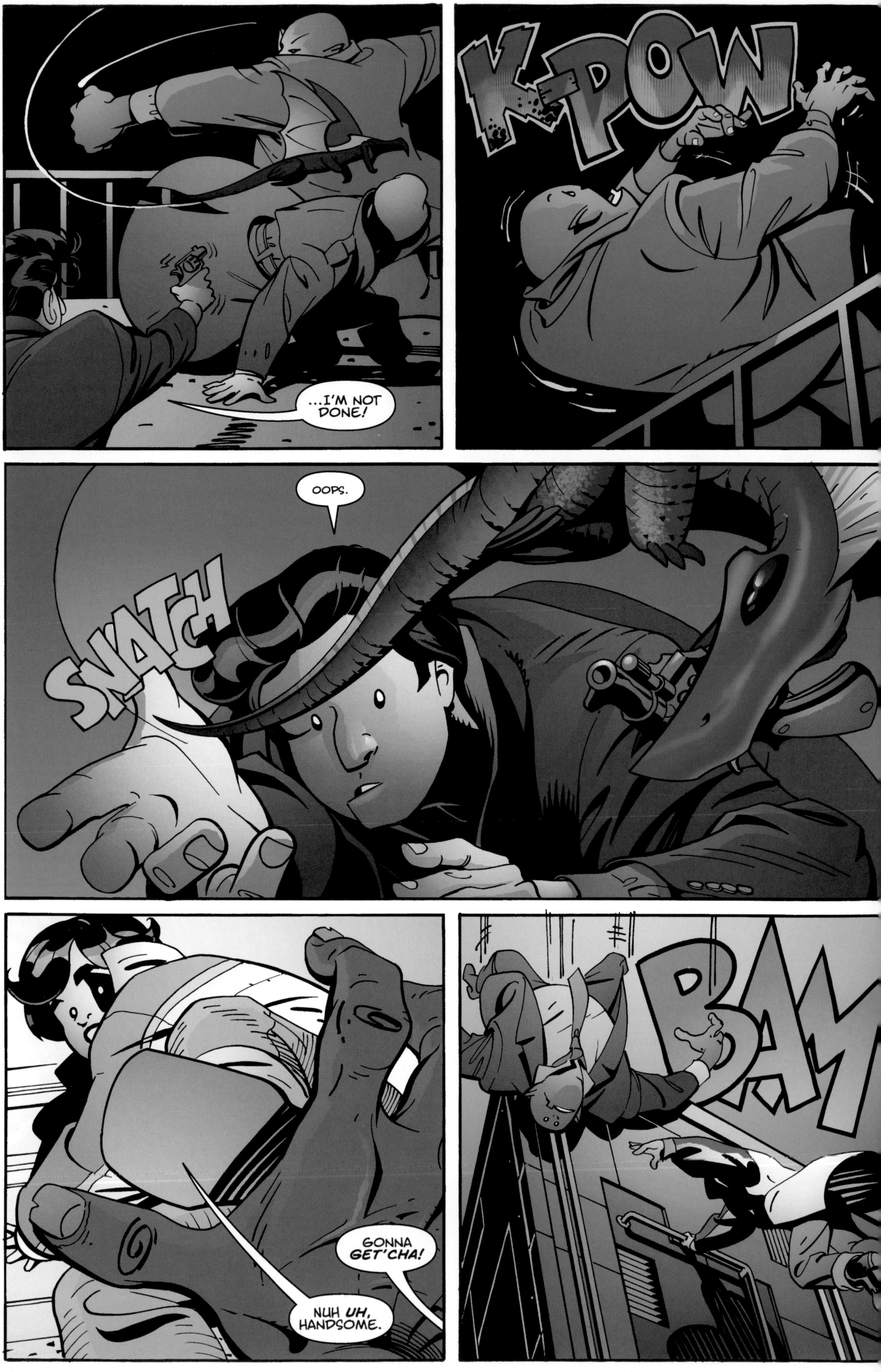
...I'M NOT DONE!
K-POW
OOPS.
SNATCH
GONNA GET'CHA!
NUH UH, HANDSOME.
BAM

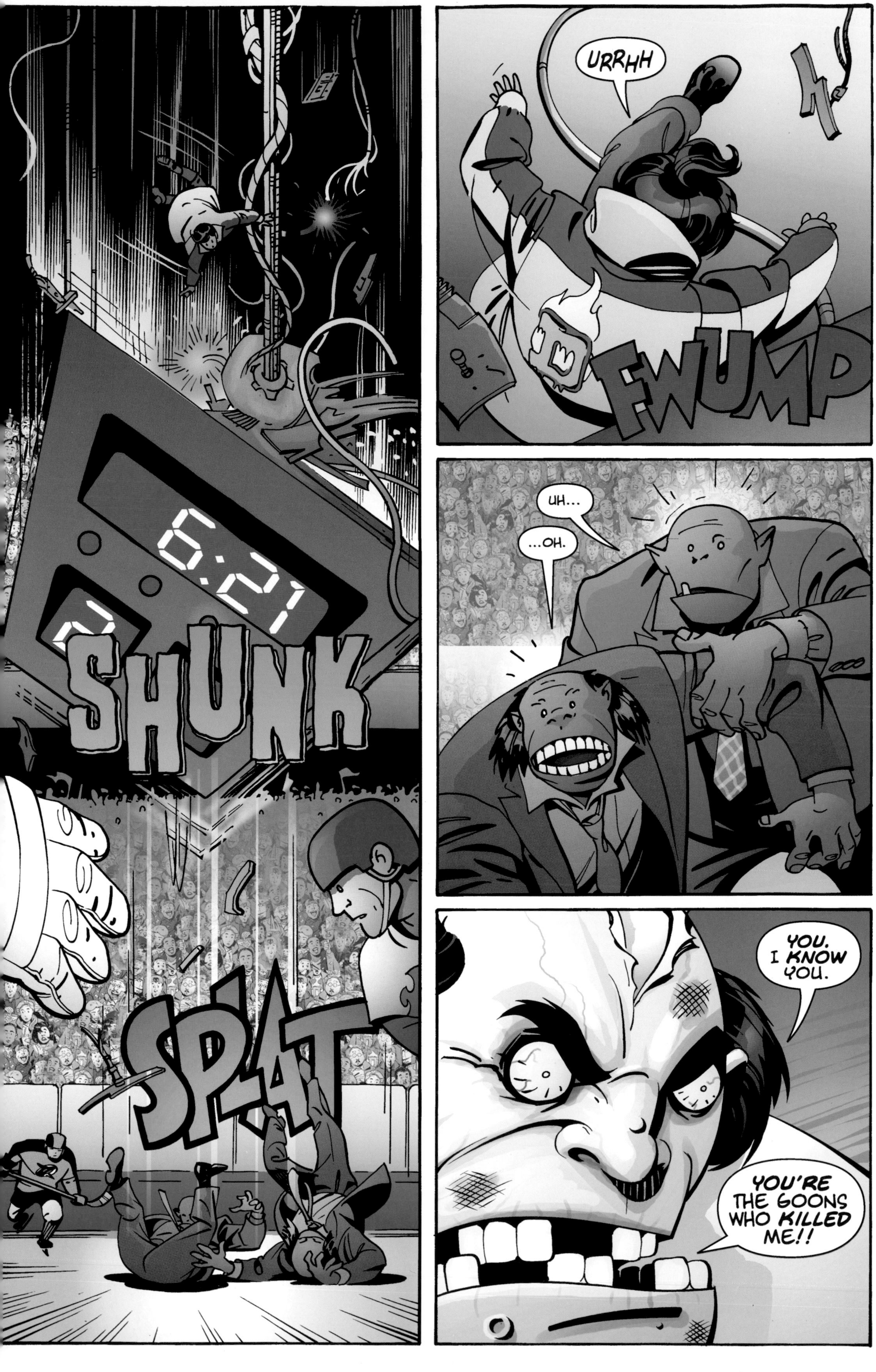

6:21
SHUNK
SPLAT
URRHH
FWUMP
UH...
...OH.
YOU. I KNOW YOU.
YOU'RE THE GOONS WHO KILLED ME!!

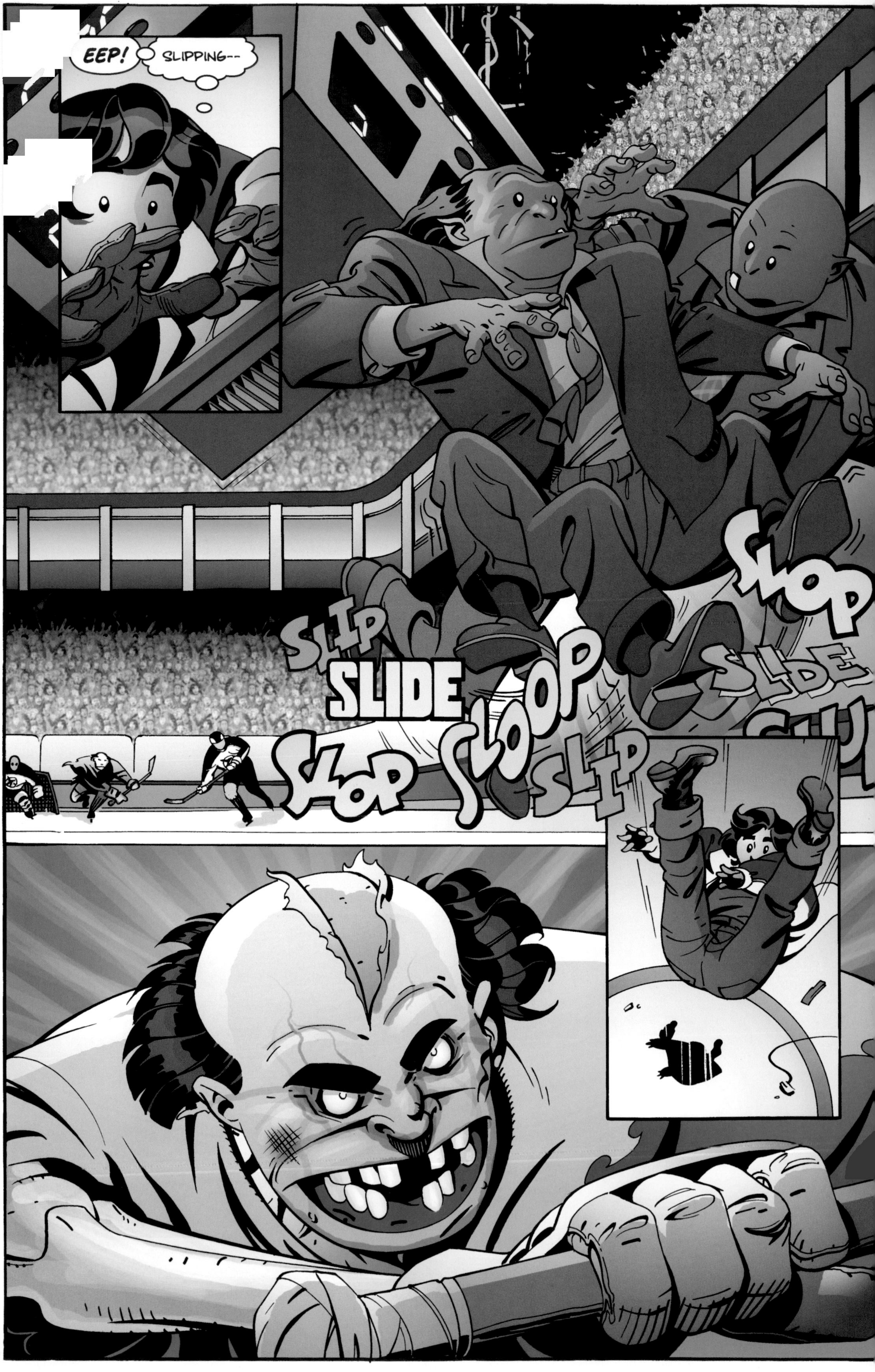
EEP!
SLIPPING--
SLIP
SLIDE
SLOP
SLOOP
SLIP
SLOP
SLIDE

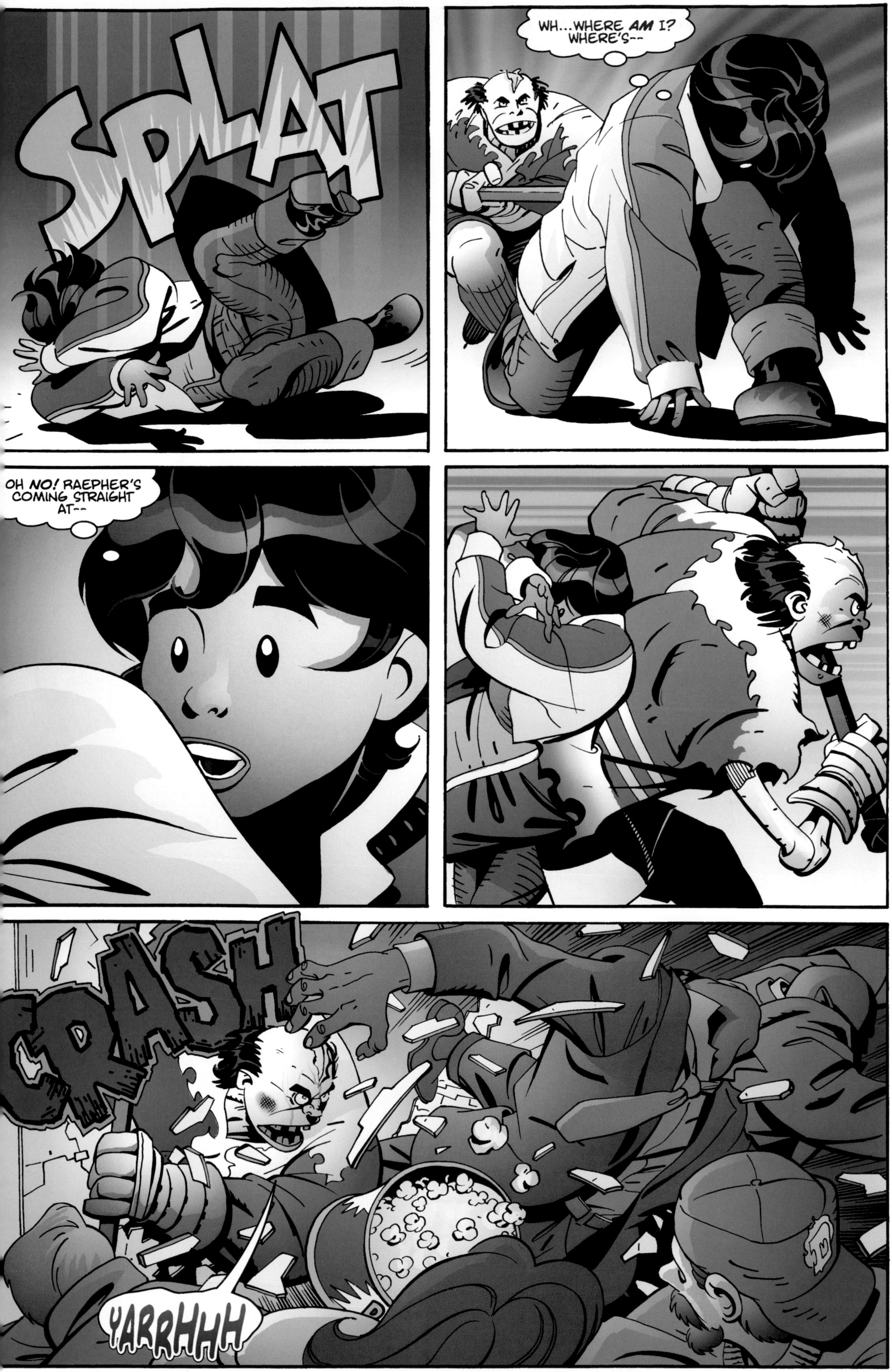
SPLAT
WH...WHERE AM I? WHERE'S--
OH NO! RAEPHER'S COMING STRAIGHT AT--
CRASH
YARRHHH

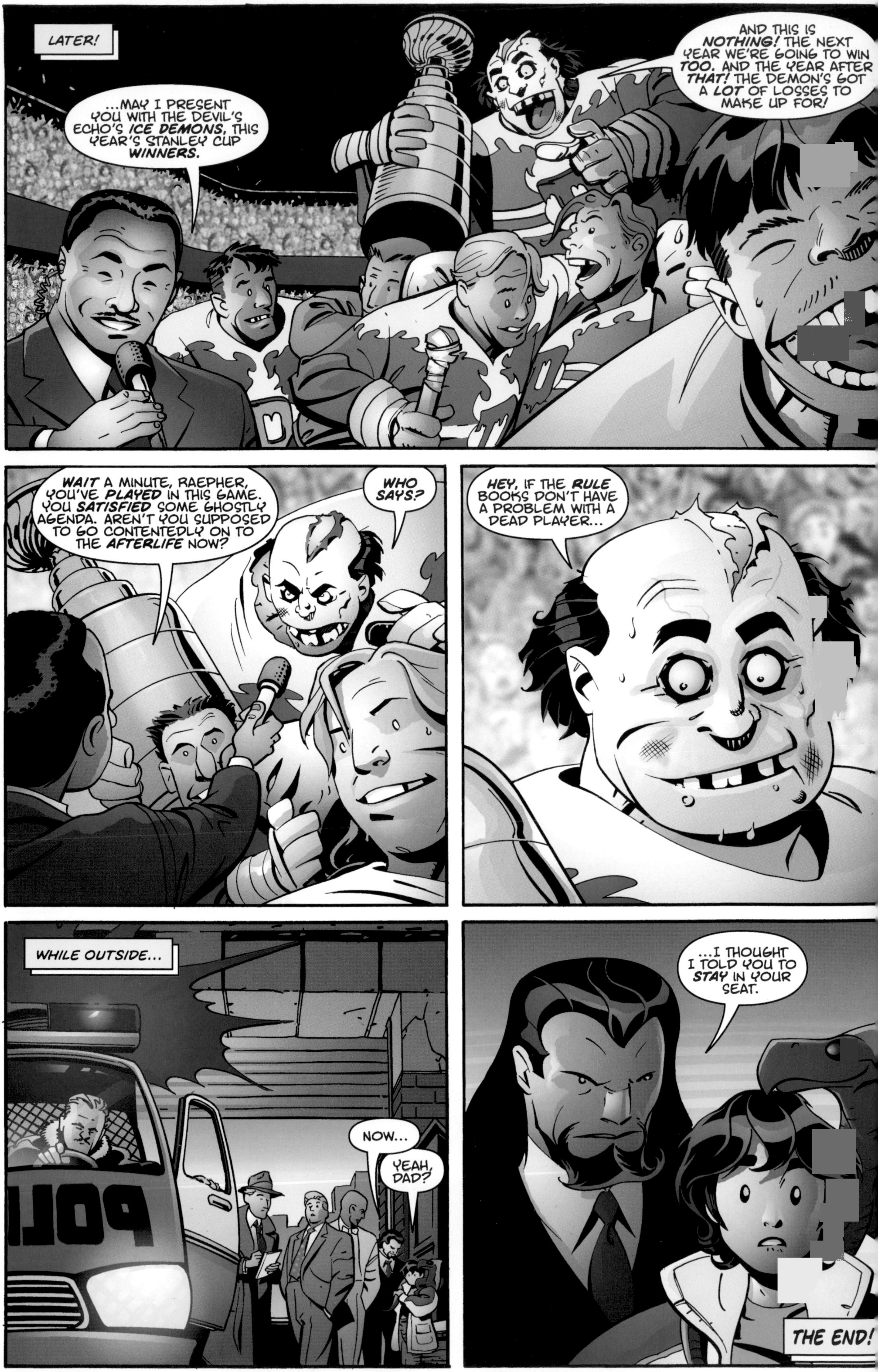
LATER!
...MAY I PRESENT YOU WITH THE DEVIL'S ECHO'S ICE DEMONS, THIS YEAR'S STANLEY CUP WINNERS.
AND THIS IS NOTHING! THE NEXT YEAR WE'RE GOING TO WIN TOO. AND THE YEAR AFTER THAT! THE DEMON'S GOT A LOT OF LOSSES TO MAKE UP FOR!
WAIT A MINUTE, RAEPHER, YOU'VE PLAYED IN THIS GAME. YOU SATISFIED SOME GHOSTLY AGENDA. AREN'T YOU SUPPOSED TO GO CONTENTEDLY ON TO THE AFTERLIFE NOW?
WHO SAYS?
HEY, IF THE RULE BOOKS DON'T HAVE A PROBLEM WITH A DEAD PLAYER...
WHILE OUTSIDE...
NOW...
YEAH, DAD?
...I THOUGHT I TOLD YOU TO STAY IN YOUR SEAT.
THE END!

FOR IMAGE COMICS:

JIM VALENTINO
PUBLISHER
ERIC STEPHENSON
DIRECTOR OF MARKETING
BRENT BRUAN
DIRECTOR OF PRODUCTION
TRACI HALE
CONTROLLER/FOREIGN LICENSING
BRETT EVANS
ART DIRECTOR
ALLEN HUI
WEB DEVELOPER
CINDIE ESPINOZA
ACCOUNTING ASSISTANT
TIM HEGARTY
BOOK TRADE COORDINATOR

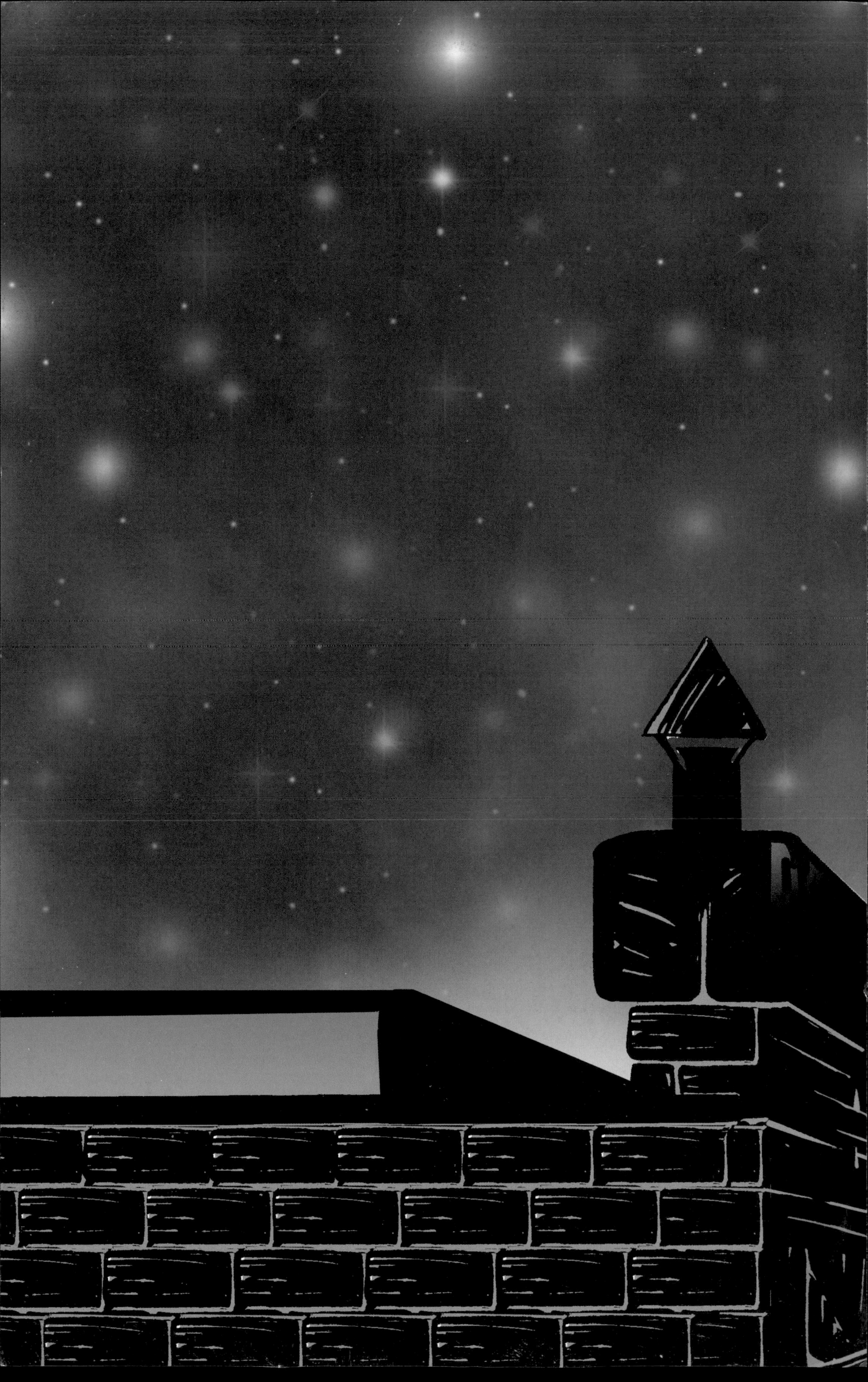